I read all of Lisa's books. I trust and love her [...]
know God and make Him known. There i[...]
ing *Put Your Warrior Boots On*...what was n[...]
son in my life is this...I'm not alone. I'm not the only [...]
fear and all sorts of other things Jesus lovers are not supposed to struggle with.
What encouragement Lisa extends to us through her un-sugarcoated call to
fearless living. I'm so thankful that these words have landed in my heart for
such a time as this! Lord, make me a fearless warrior for Your kingdom!

**Jill Kelly**
*New York Times* best-selling author of *Without a Word* and *Kelly Tough*

If you find yourself tied up in knots of fear, anxiety, and worry, then *Put Your
Warrior Boots On* is the book for you! Not because Lisa Whittle has all the
answers, although she is wise beyond her years, but because she leads you
page-by-page to the One who IS the answer. Fair warning: Don't buy this
book expecting a soul spa that presents you with comfortable, feel-good, simple spiritual suggestions. Buy this book prepared for a challenging, gritty, soul-
deep boot camp that will help the worry-torn become warriors. Ultimately,
this step-by-step, Bible-soaked book will lead you to the courage and peace
you've been longing for.

**Gwen Smith**
Cofounder of Girlfriends in God, speaker, worship leader,
author of *I Want It ALL* and *Broken Into Beautiful*

Lisa has the voice of a prophet, speaking truth and wisdom in a compassion-
ate and practical style. I could sit under her teaching all day. The truth- and
grace-filled relevancy is a message every Christian will be hungry to hear. If
you feel stuck and frustrated by the world around you and want someone to
pour some faith into your soul, this is the book for you! I couldn't put it down,
and I'm betting you won't be able to either.

**Sharie King**
Author, speaker and cofounder of Clayton King Ministries

When my wife began reading this book, she was so enthralled that she literally sat down and read huge excerpts to me out loud. She would stop every
few sentences and say, "I can't believe how powerful this book is!" I completely
agree. As a man and a minister, I can say without hesitation that the words in
these pages are inspired and anointed. They motivated me, and I know they
will do the same for you.

**Clayton King**
Pastor at Newspring Church, author and evangelist

There are moments in everyone's life when fear wins over faith, circumstances cripple hope, and defeat feels inevitable. Lisa is the kind of friend who not only helps you get back up after defeat but also helps you strap on your armor and willingly goes into battle with you. *Put Your Warrior Boots On* is a guide to living battle ready and walking victoriously in the knowledge of a mighty God who has already won the battle!

**Trisha Davis**
Cofounder RefineUs Ministries; church planter, Hope City Church;
author of *Beyond Ordinary: When a Good Marriage Just Isn't Good Enough*

I feel like we've been duped into believing Christianity is about us and our comfort, and then, when trials come and fears multiply, we run for the hills, unsure and tattered. Lisa Whittle un-dupes us. In this beautifully wrought sermon disguised as a book, she reminds us all that following Jesus is about His greatness and our joyful surrender. I believe every Christ follower needs to read this book.

**Mary DeMuth**
Author of *Worth Living: How God's Wild Love for You Makes You Worthy*

Lisa Whittle is a woman running hard after God, and in *Put Your Warrior Boots On*, she invites us to run alongside her. Lisa challenges readers to reject passive faith and to jump into the ground-pounding race of seeking after Jesus. This book is a rallying cry to be who we say we are, amidst a watching world, and we need this message now as much as ever.

**Sharon Miller**
Author of *Free of Me* and blogger at SheWorships.com

As I consider the state of our families, communities, churches, and world, I hear one message playing on repeat in my soul: "Get ready." Grateful for this book, *Put Your Warrior Boots On*. The Bridegroom is coming.

**Michele Cushatt**
Author of *I Am: A 60-Day Journey to Knowing Who You Are Because of Who He Is*

Lisa cuts through the fluff and gets to the heart.

**Adam Weber**
Author of *Talking with God*

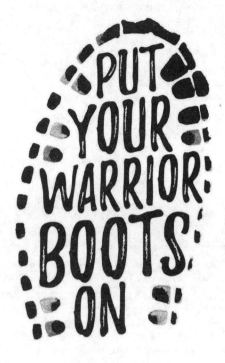

# PUT YOUR WARRIOR BOOTS ON

## LISA WHITTLE

**HARVEST HOUSE PUBLISHERS**
EUGENE, OREGON

Cover by Nicole Dougherty
Cover Images © Valentain Jevee / Shutterstock; Maartje van Caspel / iStock
Published in association with The Christopher Ferebee Agency

## PUT YOUR WARRIOR BOOTS ON

Copyright © 2017 Lisa Whittle
Published by Harvest House Publishers
Eugene, Oregon 97402
www.harvesthousepublishers.com

Library of Congress Cataloging-in-Publication Data
Names: Whittle, Lisa, author.
Title: Put your warrior boots on : walking Jesus strong, once and for all / Lisa Whittle.
Description: Eugene, Oregon : Harvest House Publishers, 2017.
Identifiers: LCCN 2016054211 (print) | LCCN 2017006253 (ebook) | ISBN 9780736969857 (pbk.) | ISBN 9780736969864 (ebook)
Subjects: LCSH: Christian women—Religious life. | Fear—Religious aspects—Christianity. | Fortitude. | Trust in God—Christianity.
Classification: LCC BV4527 .W4988 2017 (print) | LCC BV4527 (ebook) | DDC 248.8/43—dc23
LC record available at https://lccn.loc.gov/2016054211

**Printed in the United States of America**

17 18 19 20 21 22 23 24 25 / BP-SK / 10 9 8 7 6 5 4 3 2 1

*To the martyrs who wore the warrior boots first.*

# CONTENTS

# A WORD FROM THE AUTHOR

*Women's retreat, Nebraska, September 2015*

She comes to me in the back of the retreat center with a reluctant look, as if she doesn't know how to start. I've just finished speaking during the second night of our retreat weekend.

"You were awesome," she says, deep brown eyes boring into me.

"Thank you so much," I quietly say back. She can't know how awkward these exchanges make me feel—that after speaking from the stage with a plethora of words, I sometimes run out of them when I step off. In my efforts never to make ministry about me, I have gotten clumsy with a kind word. (I'm working on it.)

My awkwardness doesn't faze her. Still staring, she continues. "I asked God last night when I went back to my room after you finished speaking, 'What is she? What is that?'" The way she says *that*, I know it is about the intangible.

I almost don't want to ask, but, curious, I do anyway. "And what did God say?" My lighthearted laugh is both defense mechanism and friend, easing my nerves after asking a question I'm not sure I want answered.

"Fearless," she says matter-of-factly, and walks away.

I stand frozen. I don't know what I expected, but it certainly wasn't that. Not with what God and I both know. I want to laugh out loud or crumple in a heap on the floor, but either would be rude. I feel the way one does when confronted with irony. I feel like a fraud...because all I can think about is what happened on the plane.

*Two weeks before:* I am on a plane bound for Texas, being rocked to sleep in 15D by the hum of the jet engine and the warm sun peeking in through the half-cracked shade. Jesus music sings in my ears. *People* magazine lies lazy in my lap. Soon I drift into that semiconscious state where I'm asleep but not, dreaming but thinking…body still, breathing shallow. It is about this time the terror grips me in the most unwelcome way I have never known.

I jolt awake, feeling agitated and fear-filled, convinced my whole family is going to die. *How can I sleep when the world is cruel and dark?* I think hysterically. *Things are bad, I can control nothing, and none of us will be okay.* Everything far off seems imminent; everything histrionic seems reasonable. It is the way we all feel when the evil one terrorizes us: there is no spiritual logic or peace.

My body is stiff and my glands spill with sweat. I keep my head still but sneak a glance at the man sitting silently next to me, sure I have frightened him, sure he is feeling the panic and fear too. It surprises me to see that he sits with folded hands, cool as a cucumber, head leaned back and eyelids heavy. *How can he sleep at a time like this?* I wonder. By the look of it, the answer is "pretty well."

I am inexplicably wrecked, with nothing to do with my angst except for what is instinct: write some words to open the sore and let it drain out. I pick up the phone already in my lap and start writing in my notes.

I write about how I'm scared. Scared of this crazy world. Scared not to have control. Scared to raise children in it. Scared I won't have time to learn how to be a better daughter before my parents slip away from me. The words come out reckless, unfocused, raw and scattered, not unlike my own soul at the present moment.

I keep trying to wipe my eyes before the flight attendant comes to ask me if I want a drink. I wonder what she would think if I tell her, *No, I don't want a drink, thank you very much. I want to make all the crazy of the world go away. Can you bring me a big glass of that?* I can only imagine her response in dealing with me, the crazy person on the plane.

It is not long before the flight comes to an end and I arrive at my destination without the plane falling from the sky or the world coming to an end. But my fears don't stop when we land. For months I've felt gripped by fear, scared to death—this moment is just the culmination. I'm beginning to feel that despair is my new normal. I'm sliding into skepticism—accepting that this world will never get better. And that hopelessness is the kiss of spiritual death. My prayers of *Come quickly, Lord Jesus*, are more about rescue than the desire for His presence.

So you'll better understand when I say that just two weeks later, being called out as "fearless" sounds like a cruel joke. Of all things, it is a title I do not deserve. My first thought is one of inadequacy: *If God is looking for fearless people, warriors to further the Kingdom, He'd better keep looking. He's surely made some mistake. I'm a horrible candidate. I wear out easily and live for safety.*

But then, in the perfectly gentle correction of my Father, He reminds me that His confidence does not rest on me. Powerful is His gig, not mine. Fearless is His definition, and He lives in my heart. His call on my life isn't about who I am, but who I can be. Hope, destiny, promise—Jesus is calling the Jesus strong inside to come out. He is speaking to the authority and potential I have as a child of God— a woman who is grounded and sure…a warrior, steadfast in the faith, not a Christian lightweight curled up in a nervous breakdown on the floor.

It's the same call to you, my friend. Praise be to God, it's who we both can be.

I won't sugarcoat it: the world is not okay. Terrorists are a part of society now. Shootings will continue to occur. (I write this just days after another mass shooting.) Drugs aren't going away, relationships won't last, people will be abused, obsession over money will cloud judgment, and people's hearts will continue to be perverted and respond with sexual deviances. We can't change this, for the problems are inward. But we can ready ourselves to live despite it, rise above it, point people to the solution in Jesus. It will never be about who we are or what we can do. It will always be about Who He is and what He can do with us. That truth makes me move past my panic on a plane… respond to a call of fearlessness… and exhale with joy and hope.

It is some months later, after the crazy plane ride and subsequent retreat weekend where I heard from the woman the *fearless* word, that God speaks to my heart. *Lisa, write a manual.*

I don't fully understand. I am an expert at nothing but running to God to help with my fears.

But maybe this is all any of us need to point people to The Way.

I have been thinking about it a lot, how the state of the world has us all so freaked out. How believers who know the end of the story live just as scared as nonbelievers. How this lack of confidence and strength is no way to live. I speak from experience. I don't want to live this way anymore. I need to know how to live and, I suspect, so do you. Holding on for dear life all the time is exhausting, and freaking out constantly has us all sick to death. We need a different strategy.

It is for this reason I write this book.

Not because I have no fear, but because I do.

Not because I am consistently hopeful, but because I need hope more consistently.

Not because I have the words and strategy, but because His Word has all the strategy we need, and I want to point us to it and help us activate it in our lives.

I love us, Jesus followers…I love you. I am tender to our daily groanings, and I want to help. I want to help us find the clarity of God amidst this world's mess and confusion. I believe that God can "make [us] strong, just as my Good News says" (Romans 16:25). As

Samuel Brengle once said, "God has been better to me than all my fears."[1] Fears have nothing on a God with the antidote.

As I write this book, even now, hard things in this world keep happening, and sometimes I feel like I can't write fast enough to help us through. But then I remember that God being God hasn't changed. He is the Savior, for now, for then, forever. And so I write with urgency and the great understanding that God runs this thing, and thankfully, I do not. In this belief we can truly find rest.

*Fears have nothing on a God with the antidote.*

### Prepared, Not Panicked

My friends, there's a difference between being burdened and being hysterical. This is not a book born of hysteria; it is a manual born of urgency. Those are two very different things. Hysteria says *panic*. Urgency says *prepare*.

This book offers an alternative to living insecure, panicked, and scared, rather than accepting it is the norm.

This is a book of straight talk and strategy, since we are desperate to know the how-to pieces in our everyday.

This book reminds us of our spiritual power in Christ and defines the importance of making declarations over our lives as a means of taking hold of that power promised to us.

This is a book of absolutes that lead to joy, peace, hope, and clarity to help de-complicate our life.

That day at the retreat center, God did not call me fearless. He called out the fear inside of me, summoned me to my potential. He called me to strip off my angst and worry and go to the deep place of spiritual confidence. It is the same place He is calling you to live the Jesus strong life.

The intensity of the world requires an equal intensity of faith.

The radically depraved condition of the world requires a radical survival strategy. This is not doom; it is hope. When we dedicate ourselves to Him, He makes us into the warriors He created us to be.

So if you are weary, if you are tired of being scared, if you want a better strategy for living, and if you are willing for God to call you out to the deep places in exchange for the better, more secure life, knees trembling and all, this warrior manual is for you.

A warrior doesn't wait until the moment he or she is called up for battle to become ready. A warrior prepares so when that day or moment comes, the strength and power are already there.

It is our cry.

It is our time.

Put your warrior boots on, my friend. He's summoning you to your potential.

> Now you have every spiritual gift you need as you eagerly wait for the return of our Lord Jesus Christ. He will keep you strong to the end...God will do this, for he is faithful to do what he says, and he has invited you into partnership with his Son, Jesus Christ our Lord (1 Corinthians 1:7-9).

*Lisa Whittle*
*August 2016*

**B**ecause my longest relationship has been the one with the Church—which I love deeply—and because I firmly believe community and conversation help us grow in a different way, I have included study questions in this book. No need to buy a whole separate workbook; the space to journal is all in here. No trying to come up with things to discuss on your own; I've provided the important questions for you. See yourself as a reluctant leader or don't feel you have the time to lead a group? It's been my goal to eliminate these concerns by making this as easy as possible to both lead and follow.

Leader, you can do this.

Reader, you can make the time to gather with friends and grow.

We put our own warrior boots on, but we need not march alone.

You'll find each week's study at the end of its corresponding chapter. The 10-10-35 Warrior-Up Study is geared toward women with busy lives, with just 55 minutes every week and a short eight-week commitment. Each week we will go through a chapter of this book and study one key Warrior Boots Declaration. The study is broken up into 10 minutes of welcome and opening, 10 minutes of me on video, introducing and summarizing the chapter (Don't like video? Prefer to teach it yourself? Skip this part and introduce the chapter on your own. That's also great.), and 35 minutes of small-group discussion. If you want to go longer, by all means do. This is your study, so tweak it however you want. Only you know your group and your preferences. My offerings are just facilitators to help you.

Friend, I truly hope you'll do this study. I hope you will find some like hearts (although not necessarily like minds, since we need the input and differing thoughts of others) and gather with them to hash out this book. If it gets us to stop and think, drives us to God to pray, and helps us live a new strategy? Then my work here is done.

I want us to be ready to walk Jesus strong in our warrior boots in this world, once and for all. Let's march together.

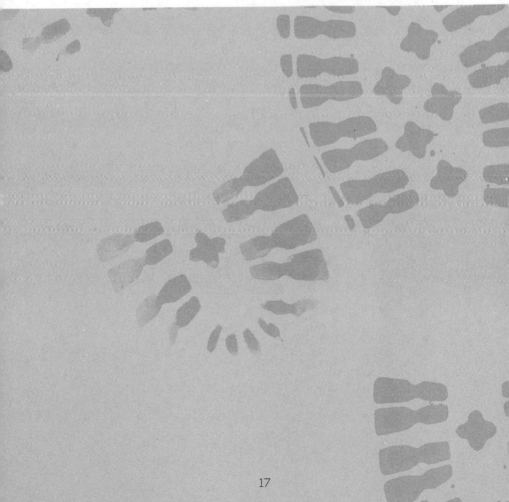

PART ONE

# BOOTS OF STANDARD

# I AM ABLE

The LORD will be your confidence.
**PROVERBS 3:26 AMP**

I'm writing this 11,000 feet up in the heights of Colorado. It sounds cliché, but mountains are my Jesus place, and I just feel more tangled up with Him when I go. I'm not even outdoorsy, really, but sometimes the need to run to a mountain is great for me—to retreat to the high place and find God in the evergreens. I feel a kinship to Jesus—He retreated to the high places too.

My dear friend Kate has a safe, quiet mountain place, and months ago she asked me if I wanted to come. "You can write there," she said, and when I agreed I didn't know that my coming would wind up being about finding a new strategy for living. Sometimes God just gets us places and fills in the blanks later, I've found. Only He could have known at the time of invitation that when the date actually came, I would be scared to death and desperately in need of Him to awaken my inner warrior.

After a long, chatty drive from the Denver airport, Kate and I arrive at the mountain place and spend the first 24 hours mostly caved up in our own spaces, alone with computer screens and reference books and our favorite worn Bibles like spiritual hermits. I am an introvert of few needs in these types of scenarios, but after a day here, I get the urge to venture outside. "Want to go on a walk with me?" Kate asks the next noon, and I jump on it. I throw on my tennis shoes and wrap up in scarf and coat, thankful I had the good sense to pack a water-repellant one since the clouds are wearing gray.

We walk and talk and solve the majority of the world's problems. "See this house over here?" she asks, interrupting our main topics only in small vignettes to tell me about each place we pass. She tells me about the woman she just met with one too many dogs and how the house up on the hill might be a growing ground for weed and on that note, how when she went through her last bout with cancer, a friend tried desperately to get her to try some marijuana brownies. I love it all—the friendship, the mountain air, the solving of the world's problems, the laughing over too much, the whole thing. This is Church, and I need sanctuary.

It is about two and a half miles into our trek and conversation that I notice how I am winded, and it suddenly seems like a bad idea to keep walking. I ask the question I am not sure I want answered: "Where is home?"

She smiles, acknowledging my struggle with the exercise at this elevation, pointing up the hill a bit farther. "It's just right up that hill," she says to me, and then she adds, "Will you be okay?"

"Yeah," I breathlessly spit out. "If it's only one more hill I can make it." And then, as quickly as the words exit, they are sent back to me through mountain echo, harmonizing with the sounds of our tennis shoes crunching and our heavy breath. Sarcastically, I preach an exaggerated first-person sermon out loud, struck by my own ridiculousness.

"Um, hey, Lisa? What do you mean 'if it's only one more hill'? What if there are ten more hills? Then you won't be okay? You'll lie here and let your life be over? And Kate has to explain to your people you would have been okay if it had only been one more hill, but instead you rest in peace on the gravel road near the weed house in Somewhere, Colorado? Woman, if you want to make it home you'd best climb as many hills as are in the way—one hill, five hills, 25 hills—since the hill is the only way home. How about this memo: Just get in shape next time you go for a hike!"

We are laughing at my preaching by this point—the huffing, wheezy kind of laugh. The cancer survivor not yet back in prime condition (her) and her no-good-excuse out of shape, out of town friend (me) in mid-hill...we make quite the pair. But my laughing masks the internal lament that is my reality. *I'm out of shape. I can't climb hills.* If I weren't out of shape, I could climb and not consider the climbing. And I know this is how it feels when you aren't prepared for the hills of life. It is the worst feeling, to do life unprepared.

We climb the hill and get back home, both of us hungry and tired. My friend, the really good cook, makes gnocchi, and soon we cocoon up in our private writing spaces again. But my mind is still climbing. There was clarity out there in the gravel and trees.

I am not in shape, and not just physically. Being ill-prepared is costly. While I sit on the couch and watch television, anesthetized by the media and pretending my bubble is burst-proof, there is a spiritual battle going on that I'm making myself less equipped to fight. I am shooting myself in my foot every single day by my lack of spiritual preparation—and then I get mad when I find I can't walk Jesus strong consistently. I want to play, not pray. But praying will save my life.

It is no wonder that I cave in to fear when the crazy of the world is shoved in my face. I can't stop it. I can't protect my children enough. Too many hills, too hard for me to climb in my current condition. So I watch TV to make the anxiety go away.

So I pick my distraction of choice to make the anxiety go away. This is the plight of humankind. Yet the hills are a part of life. The hill is the only way home. How we prepare for those hills determines how well we make the journey.

---

*I want to play, not pray.*
*But praying will save my life.*

---

As believers in Jesus Christ, we don't have to distract ourselves from a feeling of doom. And yet daily, distraction is our strategy. We welcome in things that keep our mind on the fluff. When did we decide we should live below our potential as children of God? In truth, the *when* doesn't really matter. What matters is that now, this very moment, today, we can change and live a different way: Jesus strong.

It is the call of God, the call that awakens the warrior however sleepy and ill-prepared we may be: *Rise up. Stop living scared. Get ready. Prepare for the hills. This world doesn't own you unless you give it permission. Put your warrior boots on, walk in My authority, and live.* It is the very reason for this book, to claim the power that is rightfully ours. I'm tired of our whimpering and wandering. We live most of our days just getting by and occasionally getting lucky. But God made us for more: He created us to be His warriors who live steady and strong.

Most of us weren't ready for the current level of the world's crazy, though realistically, the world has always been unwell. The news has been especially cruel to us lately, with all its talk of terrorism and sexual slavery and shootings of innocent people, but none of it is new nor is it a surprise to God. Slavery, terrorism, sexual exploitation, and senseless violence have been going on long before Christ came and continuing at a steady pace ever since. It's just come closer and become more personal, so we are finally paying attention—and as a fleshly result, living scared to death. I see us. We worship hard on Sundays, but during the week we panic, chew our nails, and watch the happenings with the scaredy-cat eyes. The world controls our joy levels, the level of our worry and feeling of security. No wonder we live much of life in a fetal position, breathless. *Hills, hills, hills.*

Where is our inner warrior? Where is our Jesus strong life? Where is our willingness to put down what makes us soft and develop what helps us endure? Why do we settle for flimsy-soled shoes when He's called us to walk in warrior boots of spiritual confidence, hope, and grit?

I know what God is telling me up here on this mountain. *We've got to talk about this. My people need to get real, get a strategy, and get strong.* I have to get real with myself. I've been frozen in fear for months. He's speaking to the deep places inside of me, confronting me in my spiritually sedentary state, convicting me by His Holy Spirit that He will be the only rock to lean on. I've been a believer for almost my entire 44 years. And yet I'm a spiritual embryo.

Out here on this mountain, I know: In order to face this hill, in order to live as a warrior, we have to change, and that change has to start with taking a hard, honest look. If we are going to walk Jesus strong, once and for all, we must see and admit our true problem.

*We are spiritually out of shape.* Many of us aren't in climbing shape. We get winded easily when it comes to our relationship with God. As long as the road stays level, we don't notice that our spirituality has become sedentary. But the hills of life expose our lack of spiritual depth. Our God-ish lives—in which we do all the right, good Christian things but lack inner fortitude and relationship—won't give us the grit to make the climb. It may knit us a warm, fuzzy spiritual blanket. But the blanket is just another thing to carry in our backpack. We don't need comforts and spiritual trinkets; we need will. We don't need spiritual decorations; we need spiritual declarations over our life. We need stamina and guts. Living God-ish wrecks us because it makes us feel close enough, good enough. And in that space, we never reach for God.

My husband and I have a hard conversation one night, one of those *come to Jesus* ones, with our teenaged son. Up to this point I am fairly sure, by all outside symptoms, he is doing well. He's a good kid. He follows curfew, doesn't text and drive (this might be hopeful parental thinking), says "yes, sir" and "yes, ma'am," and hangs out with us most weekends. But his grades have begun to drop—not alarmingly low, but low enough that we must ask what is going on. Even more concerning, a spirit of apathy has started to show up in him. This causes greater alarm, by far, because I've experienced apathy too, and I know of its quiet destruction.

He's standing in the door of the bathroom, filling up the tall frame. The eyes that I have always loved are looking down at me, and for a moment, I see only little-boy eyes and want to scoop him up and hush my concerns. But I know things have to be dealt with to get better. So I press forward with my question.

"Buddy, why are your grades so low? You are a much better student than that. We know; we have watched you for years in school."

He pauses for a minute and then looks at the floor and shrugs his shoulders. Since shoulder shrugging is one of my husband's least favorite things, it's his cue to step in and get involved.

"Son," he says, firmer than I would like but in a way I know will get my boy's attention. "Do you not hear your mother? Answer her. Why are your grades getting worse?" He's frustrated, I'm frustrated, and it's clear our son is too.

"Dad," he says back with equal fervor as he finally looks up. "You guys think I'm so bad. But I'm not. Compared to most of the kids in my school, I'm awesome. I care way more about school than they do, and I don't do bad things like smoke pot or drink or anything like that. I'm good!" By this point, his voice has risen and the conversation is on, and my husband is handling it beautifully, with strong words mixed with godly wisdom and fatherly love. Good thing, because though my body is still present, my mind has gone missing. It just dawned on me what the core problem really is, and I am silently processing.

He's not bad enough. All of his good masks his need.

He doesn't do drugs. He doesn't sleep around. He doesn't break into people's houses or steal things from stores or blatantly disrespect our rules. So in his mind, not doing the typical bad-kid things is enough to make him *good*. When all the while there is sin lurking in his heart—attitudes, belief systems that will eventually derail him. That's what the heart will always do: either lead us to abundance or lead us to destruction.

It's what I see in me too, in us, in the Church, in good Christian people. We are good enough to get by—our good masks our need. We are good enough to hide our broken, good enough to believe being good is close enough to being godly so we settle for the former and never bother with the latter. We are so good we are in the most dangerous position because we can hide in our private compromises while we pull off a Christian smile.

But what if, after all our good, we wake up one day and realize our good killed our chance at real-life survival? Would we not mourn the time we spent cheering ourselves for a bunch of precious, spiritual nothings that haven't helped us a bit?

It's reminiscent of Acts 20:7-12, the passage plucked from the diary of the good doctor, Luke, as he shares his firsthand experience from Paul's final missionary visit to Troas.

> On the first day of the week, we gathered with the local believers to share in the Lord's Supper. Paul was preaching to them, and since he was leaving the next day, he kept talking until midnight. The upstairs room where we met was lighted with many flickering lamps. As Paul spoke on and on, a young man named Eutychus, sitting on the windowsill, became very drowsy. Finally, he fell sound asleep and dropped three stories to his death below. Paul went down, bent over him, and took him into his arms. "Don't worry," he said, "he's alive!" Then they all went back upstairs, shared in the Lord's Supper, and ate together. Paul continued talking to them until dawn, and then he left. Meanwhile, the young man was taken home alive and well, and everyone was greatly relieved.

How weird a passage is this? Guy sits in a windowsill. Guy falls asleep and tumbles three stories to his death. By the power of the Holy Spirit, Paul brings him back to life. Then they all go back upstairs, eat, and listen to more of Paul's long-winded preaching as if nothing ever happened. I know believers like to eat (hello, potlucks) and preachers like to preach, but *come on.* Weird.

But there's importance here. We, the God-ish people, are Eutychus. We sit in the windowsill, as far away as we can from our center so long as we are still in the room. We don't leave. We just dabble with the idea. We stay good, fringe, God-ish. To be in the room is good enough for us.

But we tire of spiritual things quickly, and we get relaxed. We become sleepy and let our ears tune out needed messages and eyes close to necessary but too-familiar spiritual truth. And before we know it, spiritually we die. The God-ish living has numbed our ability to see that we are about to fall. We could have avoided the situation by coming to the center and staying there, solidly, all the way in. But instead, we felt falsely secure in our fringe position and lost our life.

This is why God won't leave us alone. This is why He is relentless with His call on our lives to be holy. This is why He mandated in His Word that we make disciples, and why our lack of commitment and attention to this—even in our churches—is now showing the result: people are confused about beliefs, giving blind acceptance and wavering with the culture. God knows that shallow, showy displays of Jesus will not be enough. He is well aware of the evil. So He knows halfway Christianity won't be a strong enough defense. It would be like showing up for battle with a broken arm and a toilet paper tube as a weapon to fight a real, formidable foe.

The trouble is, we are addicted to easy Christianity, and it's hard to get it out of our system. For many of us, it's become the accepted way of life. We don't see a problem with shallow or stale religion. We sit at the fringe and think it's as good as the center. We don't see the danger in human attempts to jazz up the gospel and make it about us. But in the end, *we pay*.

*We don't need spiritual decorations;*
*we need spiritual declarations over our life.*

God-ish living scratches the Christian itch, but we have to keep scratching because the itch never goes away. It's a lifetime of toil. We never develop depth. We never get in shape for the hills. We never know true change and sanctification—the process by which we tangibly experience the glory and benefit of God through the long obedience that makes us holy. Our warrior skills don't develop while we live God-ish lives. We stay soft and ill-prepared…and underneath, we hope nothing ever happens to expose our lack of fortitude and commitment.

No wonder we are afraid all the time.

Hardship exposes God-ish Christians. The hills of life are the gift we never want, the catalyst for growth and sanctification we desperately need. On flat ground, we can't see our whole truth.

Not only are we spiritually out of shape, but when we do come face-to-face with our spiritual inadequacy, many of us *waste time pretending there is a way around the hill.* I appreciate the bluntness with which John Eldredge said this in his book *Walking with God*:

> The world we live in is a world at war. Why is that so hard to accept? What is this propensity, this inclination in us, to ignore the facts? No—that's not strong enough. What is this insistence in us to see life the way we want to see it, as opposed to the way it is?[1]

Our insistence to accept our own spin is what harms us.

It is the way of the lame man in John 5, who, when asked by Jesus if he wants to get well, goes into a long diatribe about how much he needs the healing waters of the Bethesda pool instead of truly seeing the Healer, standing in front of Him, asking the question.

> "I can't, sir," the sick man said, "for I have no one to put me into the pool when the water bubbles up. Someone else always gets there ahead of me" (verse 7).

The pool gets the focus, while the Healer, the only true Healer, is right there, ready to make him well. Oh, isn't this us? Aren't we, too, professional deflectors, coming up with our own cures, over-looking Jesus ready and able to help, pretending lesser solutions can solve it all?

Pretenders will never get prepared; they will just waste their life. I'm weary of this gig—this clinging to smokescreens and false securities. Acceptance of where we are and what we need to do about it is the strategy for sanity and hope, and I want some of that.

The famous quote couldn't be truer: "In this life we are all just walking up the mountain and we can sing as we climb or we can complain about our sore feet. Whichever we choose, we still gotta do the hike."[2]

No matter the level of crazy…no matter whether we want to or not…no matter if we are properly prepared for what life throws at us…*we still gotta do the hike.*

> *The hills of life are the gift we never want,*
> *the catalyst for growth and sanctification*
> *we desperately need. On flat ground,*
> *we can't see our whole truth.*

I'm tired of lamenting about the hills because I'm not in shape. I'm tired of trying to control things I cannot.

I'm tired of fighting uphill battles with the world for my kids to turn out as decent human beings who love God.

I'm tired of drugs stealing the lives of our kids away, tired of sexual horrors happening behind closed doors, tired of liars and cheaters turning good people into skeptics, jading us about honor, trust, kindness, and love.

I'm tired of feeling blindfolded and batting wildly at monsters that live in the dark, hoping I make contact and do some damage so I can feel more in control and less afraid.

I'm tired of the news determining my emotions.

This is where we have to get for anything to change: we have to get so mad at the stifling, the weariness, the manipulation that we are willing to do whatever it takes to rid ourselves of it. Putting on warrior boots is an act of determination, yes, but it's also an act of revolt. We determine we aren't going to lie down and take it anymore. You and I can't change how bad this world gets, but we can take it on in new strength.

But this will not be the kind of strength born of flesh. It will, instead, be the strength born of the mighty Spirit of God, who lives and moves inside us—the irony of strength that comes from dependence and holy trust and rest. The rest of God produces strength because it stops human hustle. Often we create our own weariness because we refuse to rest in God. So even in this moment, let us take our tired and let it rally us. Even in our weariness, we can be determined. We can revolt against what has made us feel weak and watch God forge inside us the strength to walk Jesus strong, for once and for all.

Do you feel it? We're on the cusp of a new way to live.

## Brave Is Not the Point

Let me take this off the table: *you don't have to be brave.*

Stay with me. Let me explain.

You know how you feel when a great song comes on the radio too much and in its popularity it becomes overplayed? That's what it's like for me with the word *brave.*

I used to love it. I used to feel like it was the best and strongest word I had ever heard, the word I always longed to be. I used to think *if I were just braver* I could do that hard thing.

The list of hard things was long. I drove myself crazy with the list. *If I were braver I would witness for God. If I were braver I would stop gossip in its tracks and fight harder for the underdog and bungee jump and maybe even travel to Africa. If I were just braver.*

But then it got used a lot. It got overplayed. I started hearing and seeing it at every turn—on bracelets, on plaques and T-shirts, in everyday conversation. It led me to wonder what the word even meant. Does *brave* mean strong? Heroic? Determined? Or is it just a casual description of a person who does what other people might not?

Then one day I am exiting the hair salon and I overhear one friend say to the other as they both walk out the door, "Oh, girl, you are brave," and it is clear she is referring to her friend's decision to cut her hair short and dye it purple. Right then and there I silently push back on *brave*. I remember my friends fighting cancer and other friends fighting in the military and the boy with no limbs I saw on TV who faces his giants every day with a smile, and I feel resentful. When it comes to *brave*, purple hair shouldn't make the cut.

No, we call too many regular things brave.

So here's a new life strategy: we don't have to be brave; we just have to be prepared. This evens the playing field. This is something regular people like me can do. *Brave* feels hard and nebulous. *Prepared* feels doable and concrete.

The world tells us we won't be safe, bad will come for us, evil will snatch our families away. Those things are too big for my brave. They're too big for yours too. And that's okay, because Jesus is handling the brave part quite well without our help. Even as we're told by the world that God is not in charge, we walk in His authority. The world doesn't have to understand that for it to be true. This position doesn't change without the world's endorsement.

Whether or not we feel able, we have it in us to put on our warrior boots and go. You are able, but not because you mustered up a brave moment. You are able to walk Jesus strong because of who He is and what He has already done. He is our confidence. His strength is our strategy. Our job is to live the warrior boots life of centered, steadied conviction and confidence and walk in His power and authority until this world ends.

In his book *Sit, Walk, Stand*, the martyred Christian Watchman Nee writes that we *sit* in the finished work of God on the cross. We *walk* through life with this understanding. We *stand* in the rightful authority we have been given. This stance has nothing to do with our trying to be brave. Our strength comes from our inheritance.

> God never asks us to do anything we can do. He asks us to live a life which we can never live and to do a work which we can never do. Yet, by his grace, we are living it and doing it.[3]

That's it, friends. We everyday believers in Jesus—parents who have had children go to heaven, people who lose jobs and develop horrible illness and endure harsh, unfair things and are on the edge of financial crisis—who by His grace keep breathing. Because of Him there will always be hope. But as long as we tell ourselves we are simply being brave, we aren't giving God His proper due for holding us together. We are relying on something we don't fully understand and that can come and go depending on human factors. It's not that we can't have a humanly strong moment; it's just that our best humanly strong moment isn't built to last. (There's a subtle humanistic message, too, preached in this idea of brave. At its core, that message promotes self-sufficiency and not God reliance.)

Putting on our warrior boots, developing a core resoluteness, and becoming mentally and spiritually prepared for the battle aren't things we can do in our own strength. How often we hide in the shadows because we do not believe we have it in us. It's not true. Because of Jesus, we do. *We all do.*

The author of Hebrews tells us to keep our eyes on Jesus, "the champion who initiates and perfects our faith" (12:2). God is thorough. He's not like us, starting lists He never finishes, leaving projects undone. In this verse He's saying, *I've started it with you* (creation, salvation) *and I'll finish it with you* (second coming, heaven, eternity), *and your job is just not to break eye contact with Me in the process.* He is enough; He is always enough; He is forever enough. To have strength we must stay with the strength, every second.

There is no faith in tough. There is only faith in Jesus.

Putting our warrior boots on is not about mustering up human bravery. It's about keeping eye contact, staying solid, and walking it out with God…no matter what.

> *You are able, but not because you mustered up a brave moment. You are able to walk Jesus strong because of who He is and what He has already done.*

## Warrior Up

Today I want to write, but my daughter needs me. This seems like a no-brainer, this meeting the needs of our kids…but moms are real people too, and sometimes, if we are deep-down honest, we just want to do our things. We are homeschooling this year, which is already a daily stretch. At 13, she needs me to care about her things more than ever, which on some days feels far beyond my skill set. Today it's a movie. I don't have time in my already busy day to see it, but I sense that her request is not really about a movie but priority. I determine to go and be all in. And it's not like it's charity work; I love spending time with her.

The movie is *Mockingjay, Part 2*, the latest in the Hunger Games series. We settle in with candy and Sprite, and it doesn't take me long to get into the drama and see the underground lessons. Good versus evil, bad breathing down the neck of good. Perseverance against all odds. Choosing to be a wimp or a warrior.

At the end of the movie, the heroine, Katniss, has completed her mission and is finally ready to go home. Her mentor, Effie, sends her off with a hug, tender eyes, and counsel. She's worried about Katniss, the fighter, spending the rest of her life never believing she has truly won, for it is an internal battle she fights.

"Promise me you'll find it," Effie says.

"Find what?" Katniss asks, unsure.

"The life of a victor."

Hello, truth. Hello, hitting me hard between the eyes.

This is me. This is us, the believers in Jesus Christ who go our whole life knowing Jesus and yet are not sure we win. We say we know it, but our frenzy and fear tell the true story. How cruel for us to have won victory in Christ but go our whole life never really believing it—to be able but our internal battle tell us it is not so. What a crazy, mad waste of a beautiful life.

The life of a victor awaits us, but we settle for worry. We white-knuckle our way through crisis after crisis, flying our freedom flag but being thrown back in bondage with every hill. This isn't freedom. This is wishful thinking.

So let's go find it, our victorious life.

Let's have a new strategy.

Let's get prepared before we meet the hill.

Let's live our abilities out.

Let's put our warrior boots on and walk in them for the rest of our life.

I am home from Colorado now and back to my usual life. The cabin can no longer insulate me and make the worries feel far. As I watch the news and watch my social media feed, I sense the call of God for His children: *Child, put your warrior boots on and come find your life—the life of a victor.*

And I think of the passage from Isaiah, written during a time of fear, unbelief, sin, and debauchery, and I know it is a passage for us too, today. It's a message of determination and unwavering trust in

God—our new life strategy: putting on the warrior boots and walking confidently with God through the rest of life:

> Because the Sovereign Lord helps me,
>     I will not be disgraced.
> Therefore, I have set my face like a stone,
>     determined to do his will.
>     And I know that I will not be put to shame
>         (Isaiah 50:7).

And I get ready to warrior up.

WEEK 1

# I AM ABLE

**Take a Deeper Dive:** Acts 20:7-12

**10 Minutes:** Welcome. Share names and the one thing you would love to take away from this study. Answer this question too: At this very moment, do you think you are able to walk Jesus strong in this crazy world?

**10 Minutes:** Intro to chapter through Video Teaching with Lisa (outline and videos available online at www.warriorbootsbook.com)

**35 Minutes:** Small Group Discussion (Take the first 10 minutes to answer privately, then the last 25 to discuss as a group.)

1. What do you *believe* (not think) about being able to walk Jesus strong in this tough world? Now how do you *feel* and what do you *think* about it? How are they different, and which will help you move forward?

2. Recall the story Lisa told of climbing the hill with her friend in Colorado. Which do you relate to more— being spiritually out of shape or pretending there is a way around having to climb the hill? What's the remedy for this in your life?

3. How are we God-ish in our lives rather than godly? What does the Acts 20:7-12 story tell us about the importance of the distinction through the imagery of being on the fringe of the room?

4. What were your thoughts about the concept of *brave*

coming into the study? What are your thoughts about brave now? What does Lisa mean when she says that brave is not the point, and how can that new perspective help you?

5. Do you believe you walk in the authority of God? How can that understanding and belief help you find the life of a victor?

**Prayer:** God, help us believe we are able to walk strong, for once and all. We know our strength comes from You. Help us to be godly, not God-ish. Expose, even now, those places in our heart that aren't truly for You. We claim today that we walk in Your authority and ask You to help us find our victorious life, even in the everyday mess of this world. Yes and amen.

**Bonus Home Helps:**

1. Study the word *strong* or *able* in Scripture.

2. Memorize and meditate on Proverbs 3:26: "For the LORD will be your confidence" (AMP).

3. Write the words *I am able* on sticky notes and put them in places you will see them every day.

4. When you are talking about spiritual things, replace the word *brave* in your vocabulary with the words *Jesus strong*. See how that makes you view life differently.

5. Ask someone close to you to pray for you to know you are able to walk strong and live out this three-word (*I Am Able*) declaration in your life.

## Journal

# I WILL KNOW WHAT I BELIEVE

The believing man does not claim to understand.
He falls to his knees and whispers, "God."

**A. W. TOZER**

I am at one of those highfalutin' churches, the kind where they don't usually see a speaker rolling up in scuffed boots, and I honestly fear that before the night is over, I might break something.

I know I'm not their type. I can tell right away by the pastor's wife's face, one raised eyebrow and bottom-to-top eye scan of disapproval later. "Hi. Nice to have you," she says through tight lips as we meet, and I struggle to believe she means it. Her freshly pressed floral skirt and polished pink toes are perfectly in sync with the white-steepled building, and I find myself hiding my chipped and torn nails. I smile, with the smile I can muster, to both her and her gathered girls' night committee teammates. But my insides are at war.

*Seriously, God, why am I here?* I whisper in my head, scrambling for a sign of approval. It's what I always ask Him when I'm someplace I feel I don't fit in, which, incidentally, happens to be almost every place He winds up sending me. Clearly, this is my problem and not theirs. (P.S.—He never answers.)

They leave me to my green room to be alone until it's time to speak, and I plop down on the couch. *I don't fit here*, I tell God. *Why did You send me?* But I'm not going to hear an answer, and I better

39

pull it together fast because regardless, I am here and they are expecting me to speak.

I start to peruse my notes for the hundredth time, as if I don't already know what I intend to say. I am only about three minutes into looking them over when I hear Him speak to my heart, loud and clear. *I have something for you to tell them tonight,* He says. *Tell them, "You've come to taste food and be with friends, but God wants you to raise your standards, because you can taste and experience Him."*

I gulp hard. I want to stick my fingers in my ears and tell Him I cannot hear Him, but since He's speaking to my heart, I know this will drown out nothing. I don't want to tell them this, something so point-blank and strong. I don't want to be the one to call them out on motive, for humans cannot know. And I know I may fight Him, but ultimately He will win. He always does, in the end, after I'm worn from the struggle. But first, because I am ridiculously stubborn, I try my best to dissuade Him.

*Ummm, God… You know this place is really fancy and I'm not and they already don't want me here and I don't blame them. I'm just not sure they will receive this well. Have You seen the round tables with all the pretty things on them? You have, right? This is a ladies' night out event where it's kind of about the food and the friends. These women have gotten pedicures and made six wardrobe changes to attend. And if I say what You are asking me to say, it kind of takes away the whole point. Please. I already feel weird.*

There is silence, just the ticking of the old-fashioned wall clock. Then more silence.

And then I know I'm not getting out of it. "Okay," I whisper-sigh out loud.

It is only a few minutes later that my legs move me onto the stage. I look out at the sea of beautiful females sitting pretty with their delicious desserts, and I deliver the message of motive, raising their standards, and wanting more of God—awkward as it feels. "I have to tell you," I say with legs trembling, "I have never said this to any audience before, and I normally prefer to start out with some funny things so we can all laugh and bond first. The truth is, I want you to like me, and I'm pretty convinced this won't help with that. But God has prompted me to say something to you, and I must do what He says, even when I don't want to. He said to tell you that He knows you've come to taste food and be with friends, but He wants you to raise your standards, because you can taste and experience Him." It surprises me how much it's a struggle to say and how silent the room grows when I say it. I spot a few quick head turns from a few of the most manicured ladies as I look down at my notes. I don't wait for a reaction, and I'm not sure I want one. I've obeyed God and delivered the message. It is hard, and it is right. (Hard usually is.)

I speak the rest of the regularly prepared message, choking back my own personal conviction over God's tender, firm exhortation of the need to raise standards in life, wanting things—even good things—other than Him. It is, too, my plight. He had a word for these women, but the word was also for me—the danger of resting in spiritual familiarities and silently going adrift. There's nothing wrong with dessert and friends and pink pedicures and pretty decorations. There's nothing wrong with planned gatherings and planned agendas, in life as in church. But none of those things matter as much as the aching for God in our bones.

Raising our standards is not legalism. It is wisdom and survival. Wanting God the most is the game changer, and that desire for Him drives every other choice that comes after. Standards keep us steady and sure. *Steady* wins. *Sure* sleeps at night. Staying put in our convictions keeps us sane.

My pastor says it one Sunday like this: "There's never been a more important time than now to stay at your post. Don't abandon your God assignment." That assignment is real, and to ignore it means spending our lives floating, ineffective and discouraged.

Abandoning standards never results in freedom; it results in confusion and disillusionment. There's nothing to believe in. There's nothing we know for sure. We float with no destination. Our insides are dying and desperate, and we don't have a clue what is wrong. The more we water down what we believe, the more we drive ourselves mad trying to grasp to something concrete in the midst of a mental tsunami.

The grief of God in this regard must run deep and wide, as so many of us in the body of Christ live this way. Ministry leaders are preaching watered-down versions of the gospel, all grace and love and no holiness and commitment. Good Christians who once held to personal non-negotiables, dedicated to raising their families in the absolute truth of the Bible, are now wandering and questioning and justifying unbiblical choices. (Support and unconditional love for our children are not incompatible with living according to biblical standards ourselves, by the way.)

Now is not time for this. In fact, it's a really bad time for this, with people desperate for truth and good representatives scarce. It's not time to lower our standards in this world. It is time to raise them. It's not time to flounder about in flip-flops when we need warrior boots. We cannot afford equivocations about our beliefs. Convictions and commitment save lives.

> I insist—and God backs me up on this—that there be no going along with the crowd, the empty-headed, mindless crowd. They've refused for so long to deal with God that they've lost touch not only with God but with reality itself. They can't think straight anymore (Ephesians 4:17-19 MSG).

We live in a world that pulls us away from knowing anything for sure. And while we flit about chasing food and friends and self-esteem and furthering ourselves and dreaming about how we can be noticed and important and pursuing all the shiny, lovely things, there is a very real and evil Satan who is trying to tear apart our minds and the minds of those we love. We've started to believe everything—whatever the latest popular spiritual guru says, whatever the world sells that sounds like love, broadening the door instead of honoring the God-created narrowness of it for our protection—and it's a slow death we don't even know is taking our life. Because believing in everything is really believing in nothing at all.

If Satan can get us to believe in nothing, our minds are his. It is God who makes things clear (1 Corinthians 14:33), and aren't we grateful for His commitment to us for that? Despite what the world says, a strong mind is not a mind that thinks for itself. A strong mind is a mind that has been given completely to God. Cardinal John Henry Newman said it like this: "He is not a God of confusion, of discordance, or accidental, random, private courses in the execution of His will, but of determinate, regulated, prescribed action."[1] When confusion and indefinable angst are present in a situation, they aren't coming from Him. His desire is not to be understood in His leading of us in every situation, but to always be clear.

*Keep your mind clear. Raise your standards. Don't leave your post.* These are the heart understandings of a warrior boots believer, the ways in which we will become strong.

There's a popular song on the radio right now, and I hear it in the car a *lot*. (I'm still the taxi for two of my three teenagers.) It's about a young woman who is being hounded by a guy who's interested in her, and to his every request she answers no. Want to know my name? *No.* Want my number? *No.* No to everything, so now accept it and go away. It's an anthem of strength and a lesson in the power of saying no, all packed up in a stick-in-your-head tune.

This is the paradox of our culture. Society pressures us to say yes to everything. Yes to free sex, yes to whatever you feel like doing or being, yes to political correctness, yes to creating your own morality. But from the other side of its mouth, it pressures us to say no. No to restrictions, no to boundaries, no to anyone telling you what to do.

No wonder we're confused.

*A strong mind is not a mind that thinks*
*for itself. A strong mind is a mind that*
*has been given completely to God.*

If we listen to our culture, we will never know exactly what to be, say, and do. It's all a ploy of Satan. He wants us to stay confused because confused people stay ineffective. On the contrary, the Word of God says, "For God is not the author of confusion but of peace" (1 Corinthians 14:33 NKJV). There's a good reason Jesus exhorts us to "be alert and of sober mind" (1 Peter 5:8 NIV)—the mind will be the major area of attack. If we can stay confused, we will never land on anything. And in that state, we are led into compromise and sin. No two things please Satan more. He has rendered us ineffective by twisting our minds and causing us to think we must always say yes to everything in order to be a loving, open, grace-filled person.

The double standard of culture is to respect, even promote, the secular *no* while calling the spiritual *no* "legalism." And those "legalistic" Christians have become unpopular because they are saying no to things secular society does not want policed. We have become the unwelcome group, and no one wants to feel unwelcome. So we have started to cave. If we listen close enough we can almost hear Satan using our own precious faith against us, whisper-hissing, *What would Jesus do?* in our ears when we try to live by a standard. He wants us to believe that in order to be like Jesus, we must adopt only the Jesus of acceptance and tolerance. The trouble is, Jesus' acceptance walks hand in hand with the standard of truth from God's Word. The two cannot be separated—they are His very character. In order to be like Jesus, we have to be fully dedicated to both. Heart and holiness is the duo of our faith, always to be intertwined and never to be put into compartments. The anthem of universal acceptance is the drumbeat of the world, founded by the devil. Do we not know that Satan will twist even the very good?

> *Satan has rendered us ineffective by causing us to think we must always say yes to everything in order to be a loving, open, grace-filled person.*

I'm weary of the anthem. I hear it in conversations on social media—hear the "legalists" called unreasonable, unloving, ignorant. Apparently we who live by a standard do not believe in grace. Because we have strong convictions based on the Word of God, we are closed off and unwilling to listen. Because we do not accept the validity of every morality, we are not personally evolved. To all of this I push back and say, *No*.

What Satan puts out there seems like love. But it's all just really good PR. He, the opposite of love, has figured out the marketing strategy. What he calls love is a beautiful package that, once opened, exposes a hidden, poisonous snake.

It's the Garden all over again. He whispers, *Eat this; it's the answer.* And because all of us desperately want the answer, we eat. He knows his way around our fragile and egotistic psyche, and he will twist even our right desires—our desire to love. It's an evil and effective strategy.

The by-product of lowering standards to meet the culture is not unlike the parent with the mind-set of complete permissiveness for their child. We've all seen the fallout—an unbridled, unguided human who thrashes through life without rules. It's not love to parent that way; it's selfishness on the part of a parent who is likely projecting out of their own baggage, needing to be liked by their child, buying the false idea that humans should always do what we feel. Good parents give children boundaries. They are the ones who, with wise disregard for themselves, parent with the mind-set of "this is the way; walk in it" (Isaiah 30:21 NIV), knowing it is for the child's benefit to walk in a sure path. God is this kind of parent. His parenting plan for us, one of boundaries and absolute truth and yes, consequences to our wandering off, is graciously for our best.

And yes, *it's true*: the Church hasn't always been loving; we have monumentally failed at times to welcome all people in. The true legalists have been ridiculous and mean while waving the precious Word of God in their hands. This isn't love. This isn't truth. This isn't the answer of God to sin, nor is it His heart. This is wrong, and I rest in the idea that God will do as He says in the Word and one day make those wrongs right. The refusal to love is grave, and we should tremble at the thought we will each answer to God one day for it.

But that isn't the same as saying no because we are holding to our standards. The answer is not Satan's trickery guised in fake love. The answer is not to say yes to everything. That's the same Garden tactic; in this society with the *it's your right* and *do whatever you want* mentality, our spiritual immune system is down and we are susceptible to the ploy. It's a good pitch Satan makes. It pulls at our heartstrings. It's just not the answer.

The answer is and always has been truth, found in the Word of God.

In order to respond to God's call for us to live holy (1 Peter 1:16), not only is it our right to say no, it is our strategy. In that strategy, we live better.

*No* to the claim that there are no absolutes in life.

*No* to sin, even when it's popular.

*No* to the idea that the Bible is a book of made-up stories.

*No* to the belief that Jesus is not the only Way to heaven.

*No* to the notion that the heart of Jesus is tolerance without accountability.

*No* to the tactics of Satan. *No* to the broad-stroked accusation of narrow-mindedness. *No* to the false claim of bigotry. *No* to the guise of love to get me to believe everything. No, no, *no*.

My Jesus is love. My Jesus is acceptance. My Jesus is also standards and truth, requirer of holiness and champion of saying no to everything that is not of Him. Your Jesus is too. On these things I will model my life, die one day, and today, live. It is the first place we must reconcile as we determine to walk in warrior boots. The strength to walk in a world gone crazy starts in the determinations in our mind.

The extravagant grace and wild, unbridled love of God compel the loving heart to say no. No other movement could move us enough.

## Convictions

One hundred people living their convictions are more powerful than a million trying to strong-arm people into the gospel.

I've watched this lifestyle evangelism for myself. When people model the gospel, they have a magnetism that cannot be explained. On the flip side, trying to strong-arm a strong woman (or man) is about as futile as trying to get a big and tall man to buy an IKEA couch: the thought does not appeal. Don't try to strong-arm me into anything. I'll do the opposite just to show you your arm wasn't quite strong enough.

But live your conviction in front of me to the point I might be convinced? Yes, please. You will show me what I need to do. You will show me what works. You will inspire me to follow your example. You might even convince me to change my mind. I might not change, but I will think about it. This is no small feat for a stubborn woman who is long in the tooth. But there is a student inside every heart longing to learn and emulate what works.

I get it: convictions aren't popular. But when people live their convictions with an equal conviction to love (one without the other won't work), they become Jesus magnets and bring other people in. We shouldn't be surprised that when we model Jesus, the Perfect One, in any circumstance, it will always work. In my own experience, I've found that people don't mind if we have convictions so much as they mind when we don't live what we say we believe—the ultimate turnoff of human hypocrisy. It's where we lose influence, every time. (Again, Jesus is our only help.)

We are often so busy being put off by the word *conviction* that we don't realize it is our convictions that will save us from so many things: not knowing what to say in a complex hot-button conversation (admitting you don't have everything figured out but saying, "This is still my conviction," is perfectly acceptable), becoming easily disillusioned by life, treating people differently based on circumstances or preferences. Conviction takes care of all of that. There is no maneuvering or figuring things—we behave according to what we believe, the end. Being driven by our convictions keeps us from unnecessary hysteria and bandwagon living. It helps us treat people with fairness and love because our core conviction is to justice, not circumstances or extending to only certain groups or classes of people. When we live by our convictions, we don't have to make up life on the fly. So the crisis element of the moment, the reactionary response, is largely quieted. Convictions about Jesus are there for our protection, fulfillment, and freedom, and we ought to run to them with everything we have, grateful and determined to live them like never before.

> *When people live their convictions with an equal conviction to love (one without the other won't work), they become Jesus magnets and bring other people in.*

### The Conviction to Believe the Bible

*"I believe the Bible. It is God's holy Word. Every word of God is true, and I receive it gladly today. And where what the Bible says is different from my life, I will change by the power of God's Holy Spirit."* This is the declaration my husband heard every Sunday from his pastor, Dennis, while in seminary. He loved it so much he made it the declaration of our church when we pastored a church ourselves years later. It's such a rich testimony of a heart who has decided to believe the Bible, purely, entirely, passionately. I think of the words myself often…and the commitment feels, again, new.

The conviction of God is for His Word to be studied, believed, honored, and followed. When Jesus was tempted to break His fast in the desert, He answered, "It is written, 'Man shall not live on bread alone, but by every word that comes from the mouth of God'" (Matthew 4:4 NKJV). This was His conviction. It was the method to counteract Satan's attacks. Should we not, then, respond with the same method, since we know it works? Do we eek through life and fall into temptation because we do not reach for the Word of God? Charles Spurgeon once said, "Half our fears arise from neglect of the Bible."[2] *Yes.* I believe this to be true. And I would add: at least half our walking timid through life and not strong. And really, maybe all.

Jesus had fasted for 40 days and was hungry when He gave His tempter, Satan, this 21-word speech. In His body's weakened state, He took the food of God's Word as the solution. Surely He knew this would be enough to satisfy the hunger pains. Surely He knew a hungry body was better than a hungry soul. Surely it was the same message He sends to us today, no matter if we are hungering for love, hungering for approval, hungering for attention, or yes, even hungering in our physical bodies for the food that will only temporarily drive our hunger pains away.

If we believe the Bible, we believe in justice. We believe in mercy and redemption. We believe in turning away from sin. We believe in holiness and hope and love. And in those things, we believe, too, in saying no. No one ever says yes to mercy without first saying no to cruelty. No one needs to live faithful if we don't believe in God's judgment. No one ever lives redemption without acknowledging the human fall. We will not grab hope if we don't let go of despair. These, the right things, the God things, will become our very convictions, and not to live them will be not to live with ourselves. To wake up in the morning with a sham of a life is not to wake up at all. Eventually, our phoniness overwhelms us. In the deepest of our hearts, all of us crave a clean, honest-from-the-inside-out life (Psalm 51:10).

In this very crazy world, we have to have a conviction to believe the Bible: *every word.* I am not going to waste your time or my words arguing whether this means the Bible is completely literal or is partially a fable, as some of my friends and colleagues believe. Talking heads can have at it and duke it out. I will just say that I choose to live with the conviction and with the faith that when 2 Timothy 3:16 says, "All Scripture is God-breathed and is useful for teaching, rebuking, correcting and training in righteousness" (NIV), this means that I can literally believe every single word of the Bible, for it is 100 percent accurate and true.

It is my conviction: I believe the Bible. It is God's Holy Word. Every word of God is true.

I stand on it. I stand with it. I stand with God. This is the heart cry of the warrior boots believer.

### The Conviction to Be About Grace

My friend Monty is one of the wisest people I know, so much so that in my last three books I've quoted him. He's spent his life in ministry, and his ministry now looks like speaking engagements, playing with grandkids in the beautiful Northwest, consulting with individuals, corporations, and staffs of nonprofits and churches, and pouring into lives (like mine) over coffee on my couch. I cannot tell you all the things he has taught me, but when I am with him my mind is constantly blown by the way he addresses life, which I lovingly refer to as "truth bombs."

On a recent visit he tells me about going into a church on one of his consultations and how the pastor tells him immediately, "We are a grace church."

Monty smiles and says back, "Oh, awesome. Then I can't wait to hear about your convictions."

The pastor looks at him, confused, as this is not the typical response to his defining the church as a "grace place." Without pious disregard or judgment (trust me: not his style), Monty explains to the pastor that people who believe strongly in grace must be people of great conviction, for without it, you eliminate the very thing that makes grace and mercy applicable in the first place.

Conviction and grace and God. They all go together. Grace is the thing we love the most about God: that He plucks ugly sinners from death and futility and lavishly gives us things we don't deserve.

Grace is cheerleader chant-worthy stuff. We sing a little louder when we sing about grace. We read the books on it. The thought of it makes our insides swell. Grace is like one of those beautiful houses I pass by sometimes on the prettiest road in Charlotte—the one everyone looks at with its hanging trees and manicured majesty and uses as the mental example of where they always want to live. Our whole lives we never tire of its presence—without grace, we spend our lives on the endless chase to gain favor we haven't earned.

No one dislikes the part of God and the Bible that is grace.

And so...*yes, grace, give me more and more of grace, please.* Heaps of grace, grace by the truckload, grace as appetizer, entrée, and dessert. My heart cries to God to, *Please, help me give grace to people when they react poorly or negatively affect me. Let me give the annoying person grace and the disappointing person grace and, yes, even the mean and cruel person too. Another round of grace, please, for me, every day, because trust me, I can use it, especially when that person in front of me drives so very slow.* I'm not that good at grace. Interesting how we who have become liberal receivers of grace often struggle the most to give the gift of grace ourselves.

There is no better example of grace than Jesus. He came to us this way. "The Word became flesh and made his dwelling among us. We have seen his glory, the glory of the one and only Son, who came from the Father, full of grace and truth" (John 1:14 NIV). Every day of His life He practices grace—coming, then dying, then living inside of us to help. Yes, God and grace, grace and God. They are a pair.

*But.* We've made grace too easy. It has become a crutch and thereby cheapened the costly price of it, which, for our Savior, came through sacrifice and death.

We use grace when we need an excuse to keep sinning and grace when we need to end a hard conversation of accountability with the friend. Nothing trumps grace, and we know it. And we use it to our advantage. *Grace* has become the go-to word when the truth is presented and it is not what we want to hear. *I hear you, but grace. I will continue on doing what I want to do when I want to do it because in the end, grace. Yes, I'm living with my boyfriend and not married, but grace. Yes, I'm cheating on my taxes, but grace. Yes, I'm a little prejudiced against a different race, but grace. Yes, I'm going to get around to getting serious about God, but for now, grace.*

When we operate with this mentality, we dismiss the very blood, sweat, and tears it took to bring us the gift of grace in the first place. Yes, grace is beautiful, but it came through holy and righteous grit. It came through torture and abuse and injustice and thorns and mockery and fear and hatred and flimsy believers chanting right along with the secular folks. Grace came through the commitment and conviction of the Father and the cruelty of the cross and without that first, there would be no beautiful home of grace for us to live in now.

So let us understand that our conviction to live a life of grace depends on our level of commitment to the cross. Not on our empty Christian buzzwords. Not on our taking the easy out by believing our behavior really doesn't matter. Grace isn't just another excuse to live without consequence. Jesus didn't die for that.

Yes, it's all about grace. And at the same time, no, it's not.

---

*Yes, grace is beautiful, but it came through holy and righteous grit.*

---

### The Conviction to Hold Accountable

With the fervor that we accept grace, we reject accountability. But when we come to know what we believe, we will be convinced of the benefit of accountability and, tough as it can sometimes be, live with a commitment to personally walk it out.

We so often deny the help that could potentially save us. I've watched many a pastor walk into a landmine of affair or money laundering or pride simply because no one had the guts to tell them the truth or because they fled from the painful feedback of accountability. We fall into ditches without accountability. We fall harder than we might have if someone had warned us of the ditch. How much do we really love people if we do not keep them accountable?

Jesus held people accountable, left and right. He held the religious suits accountable for their pride (Matthew 23). He held His own disciples accountable for other people's lives and salvation (Matthew 4:19 and the Great Commission). Our tender Father healed, then held accountable (John 5:14: *"Now you are well; so stop sinning..."*). Grace-filled, spirit-filled love in person form, Jesus held the woman about to be stoned accountable (*"you are living with your boyfriend..."*), even as He held her heart, and held her accusers accountable too (John 8:7: *"Let the one who has never sinned throw the first stone"*). Jesus lived by the conviction to hold people accountable and in every circumstance did it fairly and perfectly.

We won't do it perfectly. We will mess it up sometimes and be too harsh or too prideful. We will reject people in the process of honestly wanting to confront their sin. We aren't Jesus, and of ourselves, we won't do it like He does. But we can follow His example and learn from Him. It's what a warrior boots believer will always do, preempted by earnest prayer and a submitted heart to the Master. Successful accountability is fueled by the motive to simply please and honor God.

When we don't hold each other accountable, we show our self-centeredness. We say we don't want to upset the people close to us, we don't know how to approach them, we want to give them the benefit of the doubt, we are afraid we will do it wrong...but really it's our fear of personal rejection that often keeps us from it and the haunts of our own sin in which we haven't yet come clean. But when we don't practice it, we deny someone the opportunity to be a better human. And that's not love, that's self-protection.

Accountability has saved marriages. It has brought dark things out into the light where Satan can't play in them anymore. It has helped break people from bondage. The loving accountability of another has the power, by the help of the Holy Spirit, to do just that. We are His vessel in the cause.

> My brothers, if anyone among you wanders from the truth and someone brings him back, let him know that whoever brings back a sinner from his wandering will save his soul from death and will cover a multitude of sins (James 5:19-20 ESV).

> Iron sharpens iron, and one man sharpens another (Proverbs 27:17 ESV).

And just to be perfectly clear: accountability is not the same as judgment. The difference is all about intent. We are not to judge, in the sense that we are not to turn our backs on people, point out their sin, but not be willing and ready to look at ours. Matthew 7:1 reminds us, "Judge not, that you be not judged" (NKJV). This verse is smack in the midst of Jesus' Sermon on the Mount, His inspired teaching to the disciples and a large crowd of others who have come to hear what He has to say. He's giving us another piece of counsel on right living. He's telling us that walking around with a condemning spirit is going to turn a lot of people off and send them astray, and woe to us who live with a spirit of judgment.

So, no, we aren't to judge. We aren't to try to be another person's Holy Spirit. We can't be and shouldn't even try. Holding someone accountable is love and concern with right motive. It is the desire for believers to walk in truth. It is the formula given by God to keep us each on the right path, through the community of His kids. It is truth in love, with the intent to bring the body of Christ together to walk healthy and strong.

### The Conviction to Hold Jesus as Lord

I've known a lot of good guys in my life, and Jesus isn't one. He's good, that part is true. But He's not just a good guy. Good guys take out the trash and open doors for people, and really good ones might even climb a tree to save a cat. But my Jesus is so much more. To call Him a good man is to call the finest Kobe steak "ground beef." (Forgive me. There is no good illustration, really.)

Jesus is divine. He is incarnate. He is sovereign, all knowing, all powerful, available and present, in every place. He was not just a good man, a civil servant who went around doing good deeds for people and expecting nothing in return. Those people, though rare, exist in flesh. Jesus never was and never will be in their category. In His hands are life and death, breath and body, the world as we know it being held together or if He wills, falling apart. Those hands parted seas and touched lepers and raised dead bodies back to life. No good guy can do that.

My Jesus is Lord.

My Jesus is Healer.

My Jesus is hope.

My Jesus is King.

My Jesus is power.

My Jesus is not just a good guy. On this conviction, a warrior boots believer will rest.

### The Conviction to Love

I can't say it better than Augustine.

> What does love look like? It has the hands to help others. It has the feet to hasten to the poor and needy. It has eyes to see misery and want. It has the ears to hear the sighs and sorrows of man. That is what love looks like.[3]

So many things have been written about love—enough to fill volumes of books. In our own lives, it is always love that has brought us back. We starve for it, beg for it, spend our whole lives looking in corners and lifting lids and asking, *Is this it?* not unlike the baby bird in *Are You My Mother?* who asks everyone and everything if they are the mother it cannot find. How silly to ask a kitten when you are a bird. How foolish to ask a dog, a hen, a cow when none of those fit. How foolish and unproductive of us too, to ask love to be in all the places and people we look for it. It only comes from, in, and through God.

Love must be our conviction. We must commit to it as if it is our only task. Without love, we hurt people. Without love, we turn them off and turn them away. Without love, words fall differently. No, we can never function a day, a minute, a breath without love.

Love is a choice, but after all these years, we still look for it to be a feeling. So then we, like the bird without a mother, wander about asking every wrong thing to wear the title of love. And we never get around to the choosing. So we never receive that which we crave. We could choose right love, godly love, which in dating relationships looks like waiting on marriage for sex but in the moment becomes about the feeling of desiring physical touch. We ask our friendships to be love, even the unhealthy ones that drive us away from God. We ask our jobs to be love and our addictions to be love and our big homes to be love and our money to be love, and in the end, none of it is the love we are looking for. All the things we ask to be love but aren't and can't be prove futile because feelings never measure up to real, steadied, agape love, which is not based in getting but in giving away.

In order to find love we must first choose to give it, which is the aspect of love we nearly forget. The greatest moments of love in our life will not be getting it for ourselves, but giving it and receiving the experience of that in our hearts, which is a message at odds with the world's. I've felt loved at times in my life—by words, yes, but mostly by deeds. When someone defends my character, I feel loved. When someone prays with me, I feel loved. But I feel more loved when I cook a meal and my children eat it and tell me they are full.

I don't know why God made love to be felt most strongly when we give it, but He did.

Augustine nailed our problem: we don't have love because we don't choose it. We don't choose love because we don't know what it looks like so we search for a different option.

1. **Hands to help others.** "Love is a verb" has been said over and over again. It's true. We serve people and it says to them, in the loudest of ways, *I love you.* I will take this love over a hundred compliments, any day. I've been married to my husband for 21 years, and I'm not sure I've ever felt more loved by him than when I watch him help and serve my aging parents in this particular season of life. I watch him help my dad into his wheelchair and my heart cries, *This is love.*

2. **Feet to hasten to the poor and needy.** Most of us don't hasten to these groups of people. We drag our feet. We, the good Christian people especially, will run to the Easter Sunday service in our new dress, but we will suddenly be busy when the opportunity is presented to us to do homeless ministry. Someone truly committed to love will not only serve the poor and needy, the widows and orphans, the people who need help, but will run to their side. Jesus ran. Love runs.

3. **Eyes to see misery and want.** We are a people of little eye contact anymore. Our eyes, buried in the faces of our phones, don't raise long enough to connect with most anyone. As a result, our ability to see needs has gravely diminished. People are begging us, every day, to notice how miserable they are and to help them out of it. People, the ones we see in grocery stores and neighborhood block parties, live with gaping wants and their eyes say,

*Please help me*, but we don't see them. We, the believers with the cure to a miserable, starving life, do not look up long enough. We must look if we are to love.

4. **Ears to hear the sighs and sorrows of man.** Our depth of love is shown in how well we listen. Do we hear people, really hear them? Are we in tune to their sighs or does it just sound like random noise? Will we love enough to let them express their sorrows? Most of the time we have an appointment to make, a plane to catch, a dinner to cook. Yes, we must set boundaries in life, but many of us have boundaried ourselves to death and thereby recused ourselves from the personal responsibility to listen to the hurts and needs of people. To love is to set our own agenda aside at times for the saving of a life. If we, the Jesus followers, don't listen, who will? The alcohol. The drugs. The abusive boyfriends. The porn…that's what is chosen from the void. If we love, we listen. And we eliminate the need for those things to fill in life's gaps and thereby help a lot of people.

## Committed and Convicted

We've covered a lot of ground, *I know*. But with all of it, my greatest hope is that in these important things you will not become overwhelmed by their scope but realize, anew, that today is the day for stronger commitments and convictions. That's really the message: that in order to walk Jesus strong, once and for all, some lines have to be drawn in the sand in your personal life. It's amazing what happens when we simply choose to choose. I love what actor and writer Orebela Gbenga said on this subject: "Commitment means staying loyal to what you said you were going to do, long after the mood you said it in has left you."[4] Commitments keep us from the flux of moods and personal reactions, so they remove our need to feel it before we act on what we know to do.

I don't know about you, but this gives me great relief. If we failed at this yesterday, God saw fit to keep us breathing to give us another opportunity to get it right today. As I grow older and see the progression of age, a new prayer has emerged, and I pray it almost daily because daily, I fail: *God, please just give me another chance to be better tomorrow. I want another day.* People will not be won over by our shouting. They will be drawn in slowly by our lived convictions. Let us not lie to ourselves and let ourselves off the hook. Perhaps the first standard to raise is a fresh determination to be a better representative of God.

The world is dying to see the proof of our God. We have been haughty and brash and hypocritical long enough. We have walked around pouty and offended and entitled. Now is the time to change. I deny the idea that we have failed and can't ever be better. A crazy-hard world calls for a crazy-strong Jesus follower. Being the strongest Jesus followers we can ever be means to live lives of conviction: to believe the Bible, to be about grace, to hold accountable (first ourselves), to promote Jesus as Lord, and to love, oh yes, to love and love madly.

We have it in us.

## A Sound Mind

A sound mind is among God's greatest gifts. He gives it to us; we choose to toss it away. (I'll explain more in a minute.) Second Timothy 1:7 tells us, "God has not given us the spirit of fear; but of power, and of love, and of a sound mind" (NKJV)—proof of an action already taken. Make no mistake—a sound mind is a treasure to be valued above almost all else.

A sound mind conquers fear, because our thoughts are what mostly terrorize us. To be strong in our mind is to be able in our body. Runners have to engage the mind before they engage the legs, or the legs will not move them. And we, engaged in a world gone crazy, have to understand that our declaration to know what we believe, to live with a raised standard, hinges on how much we fortify our mind. We won't love without a sound mind—we will be too insecure, too scattered. We will not be effective warriors. We will be prisoner to a thought life out of control.

So today our prayer then becomes: *God, restore to me a sound mind, and I will use it to walk out a strong faith.*

I sat with a young woman last year in the middle of the cinder-block walls of a rural jail while doing prison ministry and watched a lost mind at work. "I've started reading a lot and learning a lot about different religions and astrology...and have you ever heard of Hare Krishna?" she says to me with the blackest of eyes, like a scared cat, racing. (There's something about a lost mind that shows in the eyes.) She doesn't wait for me to answer but continues on with her plan for when she gets out: to move to another country and provide a place for people to smoke free marijuana. "They need to be free to think," she says, and I know it is not her kind of freedom they need. I ask her to think about God. I lead her to narrow her focus and atten-tion on Him...as the Answer, the Friend, the true Freedom Giver. But she is not ready. Her mind has been opened to too many things and it's gotten crowded in there.

> *A sound mind conquers fear, because our thoughts are what mostly terrorize us.*

I am never against questions—most of my own rebel life has been about questioning something. I believe in education, research-ing, and learning, as the student life is one I have always loved. I've long believed it was in that space that many come to know the Lord, not unlike when author and teacher Josh McDowell, as a budding law student, went to disprove God and found Him in the process. But there is such a thing as opening up our mind to so many things that we leave the door open for Satan to toss in junk science and popular, secular thought. God gives us this caution through the example of the Romans: "They began to think up foolish ideas of what God was like. As a result, their minds became dark and confused" (Romans 1:21).

This is where we are in America. Even believers who are to have the mind of Christ are being pulled in. We can't trust what our minds think up. We must trust the Word of God. Otherwise we throw the gift of our sound mind away.

I know it is a new concept for some of us to consider—that if we do not have power, love, or a sound mind it is because we have given them away, not because God has not yet granted them to us. Most of our prayers are for God to give us such things, but perhaps the better prayer is that He would restore the precious gift we have let go. The Bible is clear by the word "given" that the action has already been taken on His part, and the personal responsibility is ours as to whether or not they are exercised in our life. Power, love, and a sound mind are ours to access because of the Holy Spirit living inside, yet when we let junk in—what we watch, listen to, become influenced by that is not godly—we compromise the power, love and, soundness. By way of pollution, we give our "sound mind" away...sometimes inadvertently, often carelessly, always to great regret.

**A sound mind is a mind that is guarded and fortified.** I believe we go into research and questioning with good intention: We want to be the best version of ourselves, want to grow and learn and mature. We desire clear minds. But leave it to Satan to take the good desire and turn it on us. We open up our minds, and we take in all the information we think will help us make the best choice. Then we are surprised that we become more confused than ever. To have a strong, sound mind we have to guard it and fortify it with the Word of God. Every single thing we need an answer for is in there.

**A sound mind is a mind that is clean and pure.** When my iPhone camera lens is corrupted, my pictures turn out grainy. I've had this happen to me many times, as my phone sits on my counter top in the bathroom, and I forget and spray my hair. Then I can't see out of my camera. My lens is not clean, and until I clean it, all the pictures that would otherwise be beautiful will be compromised.

There is beauty every day to see and experience and pass on to others. But without the clean and pure lens of a sound mind, these things will never be. A dirty mind is a dirty life. It's impossible to have a dirty mind and see sex in the way God intended. A dirty mind will not see the opportunity to serve, but will be clouded by thoughts of wanting to gain. We can't love people with a dirty mind—we will only use and abuse them. Nothing kills the spirit of a person faster than to live with a dirty mind. We slowly lose our life purity when we do not pursue a sound mind.

**A sound mind is a mind that has accepted even that which it does not understand about God.** We will discuss this in much greater depth in the next section. But we have to realize it is not understanding God that is a worthy pursuit: it is the acceptance of His character and that He has a higher mind. To live with the idea that we must understand all there is about God is to drive ourselves crazy. Faith, remember, means believing without understanding.

We want to know things. But letting go of knowing may save our sanity. At a certain point, we have to decide to decide about God and then close up shop. Yes, we will continue to grow and learn. But we don't need to know anything more about God than what is already written in the Bible. It is the studying of His Word we most need to satisfy the deeper places.

*To have a strong, sound mind we have to guard it and fortify it with the Word of God.*

### We're Not Supposed to Know Everything

Not knowing is the searching heart's silent ache.

I want to know why my friend Jennifer died at the age of 40, leaving two young boys and a loving husband behind. I want to know why innocent children suffer. I want to know why some people starve while other people live in excess. I want to know why some babies are born into a dead-end life and others are born into every opportunity. I want to know why God allows horrible, egregious things to happen when I know it is well within His power to stop them.

I sit on the porch with my girlfriend Angela at her home, on the third anniversary of her teenage son, Coleman, going to heaven, and both of us cry. She's just gotten back from a trip with her family to the beach, where she happens upon a scene that surprises her by the way it makes her feel. Young men, about the age Coleman would now be, all dressed up in preppy college clothes, drinking to the point of barely being able to stand up, acting like fools. Suddenly, she wants to go home. At this moment, this beach that she loves is not a haven for her. It's a reminder of her loss and the injustice of it all.

"Why would God let those boys who clearly do whatever they want with no regard to anyone else, acting irresponsibly, stay here, while my son, who dedicated his life to purity, is taken to heaven?" We sit, and the porch grows quiet, neither of us with an answer to give.

Of course she wants to know, because it's all cruel and ridiculous. Her son was beautiful. Through his legacy he is beautiful still. Tall, dark, talented, handsome, with gentle eyes. You could tell by the way he ushered people in, hugged his grandmother and granddad, sat with his family and sang his heart out to Jesus, that he was a good one. The last time I saw him was that Easter, a few weeks before he went to heaven. I remember his suit, the thick hair, the easy smile. He was familiar—he was one of *my boys*. That Easter Sunday I glanced over at my two sitting beside me and thought, *Angela and I are so blessed.*

But being blessed doesn't mean you don't taste of bitter wells too. Being blessed doesn't mean you know all the things you want to know. It just means that God is good and gracious and in some cases, God also doesn't make sense, and you accept both of those parts of His character.

It is not about the knowing. It is about the surrender. And lest we become too familiar with this word, let us remember that surrender is soul death, the ache of which words cannot describe.

This is the opposite advice of the world, I know, to accept something that you cannot fully explain. But as Tozer said in *The Pursuit of God*, "The believing man does not claim to understand. He falls to his knees and whispers, 'God.'"[5]

We don't have to understand to believe and, man, I'm grateful for that. Understanding is not a prerequisite for faith. If we understand, that is not faith; that is logical conclusion. Faith is harder because it requires the heart, which is the tougher surrender. If God called us to obey when we understand, that would be a casual obedience with no cost, no effort, no need of Him to help us. But to obey when we don't? *Mount Everest. Higher hill. Harder hill. More.*

Total knowledge and understanding is not what we need to live strong, my friends. What we must have are our absolutes, our convictions. We have to hold on to them like the house is being carried away by a tornado and we are left grasping the steel beam. That steel beam is our conviction of Christ and His Word.

In a very real sense there's a tornado swirling around us believers, and it's sweeping us away—by the confusion, by the whisper that we are ignorant to believe in a God we can't see, that we are foolish to trust the old, antiquated Bible, that we are irrelevant if we don't get with the times, unloving if we don't accept culture.

*No.*

To walk strong in the midst of that, we walk in warrior boots, declaring to a needy world desperate to follow something: *I know what I believe.* Because when it comes to God, it is not about making our minds understand. It is about trusting Him enough not to demand an answer.

WEEK 2

# I WILL KNOW WHAT I BELIEVE

**Take a Deeper Dive:** 2 Corinthians 5:1-10

**10 minutes:** Welcome. Share one thing you *believe* that people might be surprised to know (funny or serious).

**10 Minutes:** Intro to chapter through Video Teaching with Lisa (outline and videos available online at www.warriorbootsbook.com)

**35 Minutes:** Small Group Discussion (Take the first 10 minutes to answer privately, then the last 25 to discuss as a group.)

1. "You've come for food and friends but raise your standards—you can have Me." In the opening story, Lisa shares about God speaking this to her heart. What do you think this really means and what would this raising of standards look like in your life? (Even if you have high standards already, could you want more of God than you do now?)

2. What does it mean to stay at your post, and why is this so important in this day and time especially?

3. Do you agree that the world tries to decide what are the okay yeses and noes? How has the world's stance on things affected how you approach forming your own standards? What about your children, if you have them? How much do they listen to the world and what can you do about it?

4. Out of all the convictions listed in this chapter, which

do you find the most important? Which do you struggle with the most?

5. How important is a sound mind in your opinion? When you struggle the most, is it usually in your mind?

**Prayer:** God, help us know what we believe. We get confused by the world and all the messages it sends, and we don't want to be confused anymore. Give us the courage to raise our standards, if needed, and always look to You for our yeses and noes. Give us conviction and a sound mind. Yes and amen.

### Bonus Home Helps:

1. Do a word study of *know* or *believe* from Scripture.

2. Memorize and meditate on 2 Corinthians 5:6-7: "So we are always confident…For we live by believing and not by seeing."

3. On a note card or piece of paper, make a list of your yeses and noes, based on core convictions. Are they Word-based or world-based? Pray and consider.

4. Determine (pray, look at your life honestly) one thing that doesn't help you have a strong mind (social media, TV, books, and the like). This week, put it away. Write your feelings about it the day you start and the day you stop—note the observations in your spirit and heart and level of worry.

5. Ask someone close to you to pray for you to know what you believe and live out this six-word (*I Will Know What I Believe*) declaration in your life.

# Journal

# I WILL TELL THE TRUTH

*Integrity is telling myself the truth. And
honesty is telling the truth to other people.*

**SPENCER JOHNSON**

There's no hotel in Bicknell, Indiana.

I'm staying at a Holiday Inn Express in nearby Evansville, with a view of the concrete ceiling and a thermostat that hates me and therefore refuses to work.

On this particular morning, I'm heading to a jail, which is not my usual speaking place. I awake early, a mess. The familiar tape is playing in my head, fearing all the regular things: that I am not qualified, that I won't have things to say, that the things I have to say won't matter. And on this particular morning, I fear all the jail things too, though I'm not exactly sure what to fear in this regard. (Will it be like I've seen on TV? Worse? Better?) I'm glad *brave* is off the table because today is not a brave day. All my thoughts and fears have me paralyzed, and I come to God afraid.

If I were a fly on the hotel bathroom wall, I would think me crazy. I'm vacillating between doing my hair and crying out to the Lord to *please, please help.* "I cannot do this," I say to the mirror, but really to Him. It is always my fear that drives me to Him, which through the years has probably saved my prayer life. The irony of this, though, is that I pray with the intensity I believe my situation affords. In easy moments, I pray less. In this moment, I recognize the need and pray intensely. It's an unhealthy spiritual pattern I know many of us share.

As I stand in the bathroom, begging God like a loon for help, this inconsistency in my prayer life hits me. I do not pray begging prayers every day. Some days are the regular days—regular morning cup of coffee, regular checking my messages on my phone, regular mommying, regular laundry, and regular putting the dinner in the Crock-Pot—and on those days, I don't feel as urgent. I'm casual, saying quick prayers that don't press me into God. The regular days, I don't pour out my heart; I check off my list. Those days, God and I don't talk as much.

The reality, though, is that preaching in a jail makes my need for Him no different. It's just physical location. Without Him, even in a situation I feel more comfortable, I cannot breathe. Daily, I am a wisp and a walking risk, just going to the oven to take out dinner. Yet when something is hard, I pray harder. I pray more often. I beg God for more things. How much it must hurt my Father to get His deserved attention at only my picking and choosing. I am like the Israelites, slipping into a state of spiritual numbness in between crises.

Only when we stop being confident in our abilities will we be in the posture God wants us, which is a message counter to culture. Our abilities come with risk because in them we may forget about needing God. I don't just need Him to come through for me when I go to preach in a jail. I need Him to come through for me to open my eyes up in the morning, walk through a regular day in yoga pants and a stained sweatshirt, and function in the familiar and normal. I need to tell myself the truth about this, which is often where our soul wellness breaks down. We can't walk Jesus strong in this world without owning up to the places that hinder us.

But telling myself the truth is not just for me. I must start telling myself the truth so I can tell the truth to others, as a commissioned child of God. My life isn't about my great career, perfect family, or living out all my dreams, though this is often how I behave. It is about Matthew 28, sharing the Savior with the whole world. So the risks are high. If I'm too busy deflecting my way through life, never addressing my true spiritual state, I will, in the end, hand to God my life evidence in a packed calendar and a stack of busywork and ask Him to be pleased. The truth is, we were created and He keeps us here to make Him known, not for personal pursuits. We can't live this mission with a prayer life contingent upon our perceived level of need at the moment. When we're stale, surface, or selfish in our relationship with Him and not honest about it, everyone is affected.

> *Our abilities come with risk because in them*
> *we may forget about needing God.*

**A stale spiritual life.** The reality of our spiritual life is that many of us never go anywhere with God. We never experience spiritual vibrancy. We never do things or put ourselves in a position to ignite passion. We never get to know Him more. We settle for a decent but ultimately unfulfilling relationship because it's safe, familiar, and comfortable.

**A surface spiritual life.** Lots of us are swimming on the top of the surface. We never seek to go deeper, learn more truths, discover the heart of God. It's like we treat an acquaintance that we want to keep at arm's length: never pursue getting closer, only pursue the relationship to the extent it will benefit us. A surface spiritual life will never be enough to get us through ours on earth. Eventually, if not already, life will be too cruel.

**A selfish spiritual life.** In our fallen humanity, we have managed to make even our spiritual life about us. It's the way of the Pharisee: to look good in order to fulfill some inner desire to be seen as the most spiritual. We manipulate situations for our own advantage, build our own kingdoms, worship other gods, put humans on pedestals. We even try to manipulate Him: to do it our way, on our timetable, with our plan for the future.

I am reminded of this reality as I drive home today, on a back road with trees hugging both sides. It's beautiful out here where we live, in the country but still part of civilization. I've grown to love the green grass, the easy small-town way, the wide-open spaces in the months we have been living in our small, temporary rental house. We moved there with the best of intentions: to move forward in our life, get financially well, and start building a modest home with a beautiful mission to take in families and people without one. We've been here almost a year. We had plans for that year, what it would look like. We had plans for what would be accomplished and where we would be once the year lease was over. Many beautiful things have happened over this past year of our lives. But moving closer to building a new home has not been one of them.

A few miles from what I call "the mission house," I look to my right to see one of the many large, beautiful farm homes I pass on the way. It beckons me with its manicured lawn, brick and columns and flowers placed perfectly, tucking in the majestic home. The basketball goal standing proudly on the side with a full paved footprint makes me smile, picturing my sports-loving boys. I imagine them playing there and how much they would love it.

*But what if that's not My plan for your life?* I can hear my Father's heart whisper. The question feels unduly hard and I begin to think. What if, in fact, I never live in the house I have planned? What if we sold most of our furniture and moved to a rental house to resolve issues with our land that never get resolved? What if I never have a basketball goal for my boys to play on or a wide-open space for my kids and future grandkids to roam? What if that dream of ministry, to house people who do not have one, never comes true? It's a godly thing we want. It's a good thing. Why would God not want it for us too?

Just as quickly as the thought comes, my mind turns to my friends Pat and Michelle, who worked to afford a house on one of Florida's most exquisite beaches. And then one day God sent them to Honduras to care for street kids and the poor. A short mission trip, they thought. But their hearts broke there for the gospel and never got neatly put back.

I meet them in Honduras, where they now live, Florida dream house sold, singing bunny songs and riding unair-conditioned buses to visit hurting church members, feed the hungry, care for the poor. Michelle is fluent in her Spanish now—who knew a brain over 50 could learn a foreign language? They had a plan too. It just wasn't the same plan as God's. They chose to let theirs go, trusting that He had a better one.

This is always the choice: to cling to our ideas or to throw them out the window when Jesus calls. It's always about our will versus God's, and as author Anne Lamott says, "[Your] will starts off easier, then gets hard. God's will starts off hard, then gets easier."[1]

Our hearts naturally cry to be selfish. *Feed me*, our flesh says every time we demand our way. *It's about what I want*, it says when God asks us to deviate from our plan. But I know my response to God's call will determine my wellness for the duration of the travels.

Our selfishness is hard to face. But it's harder to live life in chains. Dying to ourselves is daily soul crucifixion, and in that, the hardest but greatest freedom is won.

It dawns on me a couple of weeks ago when I must die to a tough moment in my marriage. I want to win. I want to fight back and prove my point. I am convinced I am right. But what does this matter? I am kicking and screaming and resisting heart submission, and I am miserable. I have to die if I want to live.

When Jesus died for us on the cross, He was showing us in the ultimate way how it is done—our daily death to self: face the pain, do what we don't want to do, lay down and die even when there's been an injustice. Our daily pain will never equal His death, but graciously, He paved the way for us to follow. His will died before His body ("Not my will but yours be done," Luke 22:42 NIV), because the will is always the harder death. To the stubborn, selfish human flesh, death to self feels like walking to our crucifixion, over and over again:

our will dies that hard. And yet we know, in dying we truly do come back to life ("To live is Christ and to die is gain," Philippians 1:21 NIV).

*This is always the choice: to cling to our ideas or to throw them out the window when Jesus calls.*

A stale, surface, and selfish spiritual life is no life at all. It cannot make us happy. It's a life of grasp and struggle but never getting anywhere. It's a life of frustration and pretense and the constant fear of being exposed.

No, *strong* is what we really want—a strong relationship with God that overcomes our lack of human understanding or willpower to change. Strength to be stable in an ever-changing economy. Strength to be okay even when we lose or we are afraid or we are so weak our bones seem to be crumbling. Strength in our core, no matter what.

In these real-life moments, our God-ish living is being exposed and squeezed out. The spiritual charade has not helped but has hindered us. We've waited for a sign from God to serve Him, and the waiting has atrophied our legs. We've done pseudo-spiritual tasks in the name of God, and now we are crippled. We've settled for quick, self-centered prayers, and we really just Dear Abby'ed the wall. We never became holy; we became hollow. We blinded ourselves to our own reality of where we really were in our relationship with Jesus... and now it's time to battle this tough world? We aren't ready.

But here's some crazy-good news: we cannot change yesterday, but we can do something different today. We always have the chance to follow a different path—make a real commitment to God. We just have to be committed to telling ourselves the complete truth and to walking in His, from this day forward.

In the book of Deuteronomy, Moses is in recap mode with the Israelites, reminding them of all God has done—taking them from slavery and promising abundance in a new land. He urges them to turn to God, stay with God, and honor their part of that covenant. God has provided and will provide, and they are to remain with Him and worship only Him.

> For forty years I led you through the wilderness, yet your clothes and sandals did not wear out. You ate no bread and drank no wine or other alcoholic drink, but he provided for you food so you would know that he is the Lord your God...Therefore, obey the terms of this covenant so that you will prosper in everything you do (Deuteronomy 29:5-6,9).

God wants honor. He wants commitment. He wants gratitude. He wants wild, devoted love. He wants to be first. He wants them to remember. He wants them to be honest with themselves about their heart condition.

He wants the same things of us today.

## The Best Choice Test

Sometimes we all just need to stage our own personal intervention; give a little come-to-Jesus tough love to ourselves. I call this "owning our stuff," and I ask you, even now, to give it a try. For the believer, the power of the Holy Spirit gives us the ability to hold ourselves accountable through truthful introspection. Most of the time it's just about being purposeful and slowing down long enough to wrestle over something. It's about taking time to consider, to weigh the consequences.

Yes, that moment we get honest is often painful. But it's not the truth that hurts us—it's the decision that led us down the wrong path. God is truth, and nothing of God will ever cause hurt. So don't fear the truth. Fear the sin the truth exposes. As James 1:15 reminds us, "Sin, when it is full-grown, gives birth to death" (NIV).

When we are willing to pause for a few moments, ask ourselves the hard questions, and tell ourselves the truth, we build up spiritual strength. It may feel uncomfortable and inconvenient at first. But lies lead to weakness, and we don't have time to be weak.

If in every circumstance we pause after prayer and give ourselves the Best Choice Test with a truthful response, we will keep ourselves accountable and potentially keep ourselves from roads to destruction.

**Question 1: Is this wise?**

**Question 2: Is this about me?**

**Question 3: Is this God's best?**

**Is this wise?** The decisions you are making in this circumstance—are they wise? Has God led you to them clearly through prayer and Bible reading and the endorsement of spiritual accountability partners and authorities? Does the decision make your soul well? The questions are not "Do I want it? Is it my right to have it? Is it something a lot of other people do?" Pursuing wisdom first will ultimately keep us out of a lot of trouble. Proverbs 4:7 says it simply and brilliantly: "Getting wisdom is the wisest thing you can do! And whatever else you do, develop good judgment."

**Is this about me?** It's not that God doesn't want us to have our heart desires. Psalm 145:19 promises, "He grants the desires of those who fear him." But He doesn't want us to have those desires in lieu of obedience to Him. Many of us struggle to differentiate between temporal, worldly desires (momentary flesh wants) and true heart desires (godly longings when the heart is right with God) because the world is loud and good at convincing us that our every strong longing comes from the heart. (The flesh desire can be obnoxiously strong.) So many of our decisions are about us: what we want, what we think is best, what we feel we need in a moment of frenzy, what we believe we deserve and are entitled to. But decisions based on selfish desires will put us and other people at risk. Decisions based on God's will lead us to peace and joy.

One of the most difficult things we are challenged by as self-consumed humans in this society is how we respond to controversy, control our urges and tongues, move forward when we are hurt or compelled by our idea of justice. In this life, one sure thing we can count on is others being out of our control and our being forced to maneuver how we handle that frustration. But as we search for the best responses and what to say and do in our valiant human efforts, the Bible, as always, gives us the bottom-line best approach and counsel on not making things about us from the example of Paul and his missionary companions: "Whatever we do, it is because Christ's love controls us" (2 Corinthians 5:14). If we do things only under the control of Christ's love, we will never go wrong. This is true of response, behavior, words, pursuits—*everything.*

**Is this God's best?** Emphasis on the word *best.* We can choose from a lot of things every day. We can make many decisions. There are even good things to choose from, and that gets more confusing. But for the believer in Jesus Christ, we are to be in pursuit of His best. He didn't go halfway for us; we can't go halfway for Him. We won't be perfect, and we won't make perfect decisions. But we must be praying for His best, asking for His best, not being willing to settle for something that looks good but we know in our hearts is not the best. It's tough to forgo the good for the best. But in the end, the good won't be good enough. It will be as bad as the bad if it's not God's best.

> The power of the Holy Spirit gives us the
> ability to hold ourselves accountable
> through truthful introspection.

This Best Choice Test is not magical. It's accountability for ourselves, forcing us to slow down and ask the tough questions. It's not always our first choice, but as most of us know from our own lives, it's much easier to live by truth from the beginning than it is to get into a mess and then finally commit to truth and have to dredge it out. That's harder, uglier, uphill. So, at the core, a commitment to tell ourselves the truth from the very start is a gift we give ourselves.

But even when we do not live a life of truth from the beginning, He offers us a way to return to Him and make a fresh commitment.

> If…you and your children return to the LORD your God, and if you obey with all your heart and all your soul all the commands I have given you today, then the LORD your God will restore your fortunes. He will have mercy on you and gather you back from all the nations where he has scattered you (Deuteronomy 30:2-3).

*Come back with a whole heart and be faithful now*, He says to them. *Then I will restore*. I don't know about you, but in my daily life, I walk around in need of this.

The Lord continues to speak in the next verse: "Even though you are banished to the ends of the earth, the LORD your God will gather you from there and bring you back again." He's saying, *Yes, you're far gone. Yes, you are lost. But I will pursue you, track you down, and bring you back from your living death into a life abundant.* Oh, that Jesus goes this far. Oh, that He tracks us down. I don't deserve this in my life. I've lied too many times, denied too much, lived selfish and scared to death. But because of God, I have a chance. You have a chance too—to live with a new standard for truth and watch God make you a new kind of strong.

## Growing Up

"We have an epidemic of Christians never wanting to grow up," my pastor says, and it hits home.

I see a lot of us doing this. We have made compromise after compromise, accepting more of culture and less of Jesus. We love the world and don't crave heaven.

I see us reading the books that make us feel like we are okay, we are enough, we just need to get this one more little thing under control and we will finally be in our very best place. If we could just learn to tidy our house better. If we could just learn to control our tongue. If we could just learn to believe we are beautiful and we have a story to tell…These are the things that will finally change us. I can't help but believe that were we to just pursue God, so many of these human issues would fall away or diminish by the internal transformation that naturally develops. Tozer again said it best: "As God is exalted to the right place in our lives, a thousand problems are solved all at once."[2]

It's not that we don't need to change certain aspects of our life. It's good and important to live a life of discipline and gain the right identity. It's good to pursue better, more cleaned-up versions of ourselves—the journey to transformation we will always be on. But we need to stop throwing out surface topics as the answer for a best life when the real question is what do we intend to do about this inconsistent God problem we have? Perhaps it's deeper than a messy house. Perhaps we don't want God more than our things. Perhaps we don't want to grow up and we are selfish. Maybe we want to get away with what we can and still go to heaven, stay spoon-fed and young, not know any better, live in denial of our sin.

We're in a tough battle, and that battle needs grown-ups. It's time to grow up and be honest with ourselves.

And what does growing up look like for the believer? It looks different for all of us in our differing and unique situations, but at the core it's the same. Sin, confession, and repentance. A commitment to stop doing what keeps us from God. Getting up off the couch and refusing to stay comfortable. Being honest with ourselves and with God. Prayer. Immersion in God's Word. Service to those who can do nothing for us. Denial of self, deference to God. A purposeful pursuit of holiness, no matter what it takes.

We don't have to grow up, of course. We have a choice, and we can choose to go the self-help route, do the social Christian life, talk about topics instead of the real heart problems. We can live like unbelievers but spiritually amp it up when we need to look good.

But this choice will have a result too. A choice to stay spiritually immature is a choice to stay soft and ill-equipped.

*We're in a tough battle, and that
battle needs grown-ups.*

I believe there comes a time, and the time is now, when we have to develop non-negotiables and say, "This I will not do for any reason," whatever the "this" is in our lives. (Most of us already know our area of struggle.) Whatever takes us away from the pursuit of holiness has to go, no matter how appealing. Whatever is not truth is not welcome. Following Jesus requires a *not for any reason* tenacity and commitment—a line in the sand life. Without the choice for it, we will eventually fall and fail.

And yes, we can keep rolling around in surface topics so we don't have to face the deep-down things. But we won't grow. And we won't become strong. And we won't be able to help anyone else come to the saving knowledge of Jesus Christ, which is the entire point of why we are all here.

It is our responsibility, our right, our call to tell the truth to ourselves first, and then tell the truth to others. It is the way of Jesus, the warrior boots way of a strong soul and heart.

## When It Gets Dark (The Truth about Maps and Lamps)

On a certain Sunday my friend Teri is preaching a hard message, but one by which she is compelled, from the book of Revelation. On this particular day, an older, suited gentleman is scheduled to visit the church as a special guest—a Gideon, they call him—to take the stage and talk to the people about how to support the good Gideon work that puts those Bibles in hotel drawers, among other things.

It makes her nervous.

She knows that she is going to preach something that not everyone wants to hear. She knows it is not necessarily special-guest friendly. And she knows, as all preachers do, that the trembling comes before the delivery, and especially today, how the message will be received, she is unsure. And all of this makes her feel small.

It is after the Gideon's words and a song in between that it is Teri's turn to take the mic. She preaches, like the Lord has commissioned her, and though it is hard, after it is done, the peace of God moves with her to her front-row seat. She trusts she has delivered the message well and rests in the knowledge she has obeyed God. But still, of human opinion she is aware. She bows her head and melds into the sound of worship as the band plays a song. It is about this time she feels strong hands grip her shoulders, and she raises her head and opens her eyes to see the Gideon man looking straight at her.

"You keep preaching, young lady," he says. "Because when it gets dark, people are going to need to know where to go to find truth." And with that, he releases her and reclaims his seat.

She tells me this whole thing while we are sipping hot chais in the middle of Starbucks, and there, while I am still processing, she tells me something else. "I believe this is also a word for you, Lisa," she says, and I immediately feel both scared and sure, because I know in my gut she's right. Preaching truth is so very important but rarely makes people popular. But the darker it gets, the more the search is on for truth and answers—the one Answer that will save us all.

Even as I write this book, I know I am talking about some things we won't want to hear and the desire to be popular instead is a sneaky, persistent pull. Yet I also know: the Gideon was right. The message he gave was not just for Teri or me or the preachers. It is a message for every believer in Jesus Christ. For you. For us all.

*Jesus people, put your warrior boots on.*

It's gotten dark. People are asking every day where to go to find truth. They are going into bars and asking and going into malls and asking and going on vacation and asking and going to work and asking and sometimes, though fewer and fewer it seems, going to church and asking too. They are looking into wine bottles and asking, *Are you the truth?* They erase their bad day away by going shopping and asking their bags of new things to be the answer and going into relationships and begging people of mere heartbeat and skin to *finally, oh please, be the truth to complete my broken life.*

And it's going to take all the preachers to point the people to the truth.

> *The darker it gets, the more the search is on for truth and answers—the one Answer that will save us all.*

It's going to take the preachers of the classroom they call teachers and the preachers in the carpool line they call dads and moms and the preachers in the cubicles at work they call employees and the preachers on the college campuses they call students and the preachers in the neighborhoods they call neighbors and the preachers in us all who are believers in Jesus Christ. It's too dark and too vast for only a few of us to preach.

And in this space, may our preaching not be done from pedestals but from trenches, and with understanding that we who know the truth have not always lived the best example so we have some future better living to do. I can't help but think it is a deeper grief for the Father—that we know Him and still live as fearful, terrified, and insecure as all the rest. He meant for us to live better than that.

We who know the truth about how this whole thing turns out… we who know who holds the power…we who know how to combat fear and survive life's crushing turbulence…*we who know* must tell people the truth. If we do not tell them, we do not love them. If we do not tell them, we do not love God. He hasn't given us the option. He's equipped us with the survival knowledge and skills to get through this life's mess, and when we do not share what we know, we let people walk around lifeless. This is not the life of a true believer with the servant's heart. Let us not walk around saying we love people if the ultimate love is to tell them about the One who Saves, yet most of us never do.

Death is an inevitability.

Death without Jesus is a possibility.

Death knowing the Lord is a life saved.

In this space of telling others about Christ, I must change my perspective from angst (over their reaction) and guilt (for not doing it as often as I should) to a feeling of urgency, because I am the one God chose to help save a life. He saved us first. And then He equipped us to help save others. This is a huge role He is asking us to play in life.

When Jesus saved us, theoretically speaking, He gave us a map for one hand and a lamp for the other so we would know where to go (see Psalm 119). We can't get out of this mess we call life without the lamp and map. It's too complicated and dark. We can't lead others out either. We don't want to bother the people, we say. We don't want to judge. We don't know how they will react. Maybe they are okay. Maybe they are all good. Let them believe what they want to believe—they may not believe there is any real problem so maybe there isn't. And all the while, the house burns down around them, and we saw the smoke and didn't help get them out.

For our guidelines in this, we turn, again, to the Word. Acts 20:19-32 is a beautiful reminder from the example of the preacher, Paul, of just how to preach Jesus. I encourage you to read the passage for yourself later, but for now, here is my summarized takeaway.

1. Do God's work humbly and with tears (verse 19).

2. Don't shrink back from telling the truth—in public and in the home (verse 20).

3. There is but one message: turn from sin, turn to God (verse 21).

4. Life is worthless without obedience to God and sharing the gospel message (verse 24).

5. Some of you "will rise up and distort the truth in order to draw a following" (verse 30).

6. The message of Jesus is always hope ("the message of His grace that is able to build you up and give you an inheritance") [verse 32].

Paul knew, and we know it too, that it's time for all the preachers to preach—with our lives, our hands, our eyes, our hearts, and yes, sometimes with our mouths, too. We may feel like we are doing people a favor by leaving them alone. But we are really just proving to them we don't love them. We want our friends to tell us when we have food in our teeth, when our breath is bad, and when we have clingy toilet paper attached to our shoe. If they don't tell us, we wonder what kind of a friend they are and how much they care to let us walk around unaware. When people don't speak truth to me, I question how much they really love me—otherwise why would they withhold the information I need to know? Why, indeed, would we withhold the most important, life-saving truth from a dark world?

We've got to tell ourselves the truth and tell the truth to others. If we take Jesus seriously and love people, we will.

It's gotten dark out there, desperately dark. People are asking every single day where they should go to find truth.

And you and I already know.

WEEK 3

# I WILL TELL THE TRUTH

**Take a Deeper Dive:** Deuteronomy 29; Ephesians 4:17-32

**10 minutes:** Welcome. Tell the truth about one thing you don't like people to know (funny or serious).

**10 Minutes:** Intro to chapter through Video Teaching with Lisa (outline and videos available online at www.warriorbootsbook.com)

**35 Minutes:** Small Group Discussion (Take the first 10 minutes to answer privately, then the last 25 to discuss as a group.)

1. Do you think we get too confident in our daily grind and abilities and tend to forget how much we need God?

2. Which do you think Christians overall struggle with most in our spiritual lives: being stale, surface, or selfish?

3. What do you think when someone tells you the truth? Do you receive it well? What do you think when someone doesn't tell you the truth?

4. Revisit the Best Choice Test. How do you think these three questions could change the way you make decisions?

5. Talk about the idea that God has given us a map and lamp to show us exactly which way to go. What does that mean to us who live in a world that seems to be dark and unclear? Do you believe we are utilizing the tools we have? Why or why not?

**Prayer:** God, help us to be people of truth—to tell the truth first to ourselves and then to others. Forgive us for getting too confident in our daily life and forgetting how desperately we need You. We don't want to be stale, surface, and selfish with You. Do the heart cleanse You need to do so we can utilize what You've given us in this dark and crazy world. Yes and amen.

**Bonus Home Helps:**

1. Do a word study of *truth* from Scripture.

2. Memorize and meditate on Ephesians 4:25: "So stop telling lies. Let us tell our neighbors the truth, for we are all parts of the same body."

3. On a piece of paper or in your journal, write down the top five closest people to you in your life. Beside their name write "very truthful," "partially truthful," or "not truthful" to reflect how they are overall with you. Pray and thank God for the truthful ones and for God to help you reevaluate your less than truthful ones to know what steps to take next. (If they are not family members, really ask yourself why they are in your life.)

4. On a scale of 1-10, where are you on the truth scale in these areas, with yourself, with others, with God. Write down three new "truth" declarations—one about you, one about others, one about God, and then pray over each one.

5. Ask someone close to you to pray for you to tell the truth and live out this five-word (*I Will Tell the Truth*) declaration in your life.

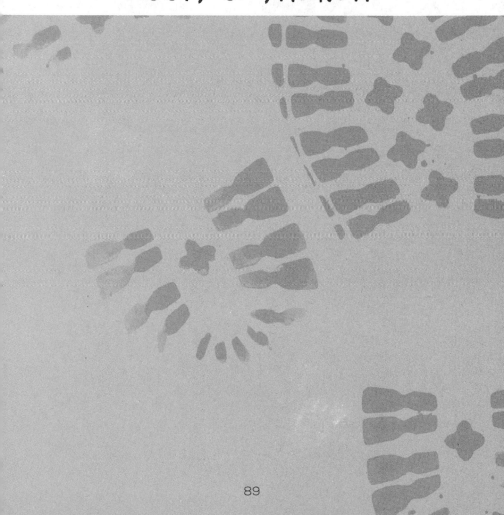

PART TWO

# BOOTS OF STRENGTH

# I WILL RISE UP AND STAND FIRM

*We will rise up and stand firm.*
**PSALM 20:8**

**H**ead down and sweating above the upper lip, I am standing in my kitchen, chopping at the ground beef with my spatula like a fool.

If anyone comes in and sees me, they will think I have lost my mind over browning meat.

But today I have heard news that breaks my heart. The tears are close; the news has made me angry.

One of my son's friends, a boy who has grown up coming to hangouts at my house, has been kicked out of school for selling drugs.

I love this boy. I call him one of my babies, though he towers over me at 18. He is a boy who smiles and calls me Mrs. Whittle and says "yes, ma'am" and "no, ma'am" when I ask him questions.

I knew he had a tough life. I knew he missed his dad, who died too young. But I didn't know drugs had lured him.

"You cannot have that boy," I say out loud, tears now rolling down my cheeks. I am talking to the stove, talking to the devil. I know he's the one who's after him. I know he's been breathing down his neck. I know he wants to steal a good life from him, kill his potential, destroy his mind and his relationship with God, and break his mother's heart because this is what Satan does for a living.

91

I have heard this story over and over again, and I'm sick to death of it. Another talented, God-breathed soul with a limitless future stuck in a web of earthly entanglements that will alter the course of his life.

My anger takes me aback. I expect the sadness. I expect the tears. I don't expect the mad. But my sadness has taken me here, to the manic food chopping and yelling out loud at the devil. With deep love often comes a rising up, and this is where I am. I am fighting for this kid and my kids and all the kids whom Satan wants to take down with drugs and sex and alcohol and porn and self-harm and eating disorders and violence and apathy and entitlement and mind games. All my heart and soul and love is rising up within me and crying out.

Without good reason, my mind flashes to a scene from the third *Rocky* movie.

Rocky's beloved trainer, Micky, has died. Rocky is broken-hearted, and for a while he considers giving up boxing. But eventually he puts on the gloves and gets in the ring again. Clubber Lang is his opponent, a big dude with a big mouth. Clearly the underdog, the fight begins and Rocky starts to take some hits. It doesn't look good. His new trainer, Apollo Creed, is worried: "He's getting killed out there," he says to Paulie, Rocky's brother-in-law.

But Paulie knows Rocky better and sees something different— that fighting-back look, that tide turning, the fierce strength rising within. He responds to Apollo confidently: "Oh, no, no, no. He's not getting killed. He's getting mad." Rocky *is*. He *does*. He punches back. And he wins.

Rocky wins for himself—to prove to every disbeliever and to himself that it can be done. But he wins too, because a fierce love compels him. He loves Micky. From the depths of his heart, he fights for him.

It is always the love that compels us to rise up and fight.

Walking Jesus strong once and for all requires those of us who love Jesus and love the gospel and love this world's kids to rise from our complacency and comfort and denial and get mad. We can't lie down and quit. We can't be confused about our standards. We have to rise up.

In my everyday wife and mom life I am not brave and I am not gutsy. If I am strong it is because I have just decided to fight back on behalf of those I love and because the love of my Savior compels me. (Remember 1 Corinthians 5:14 from the chapter before?) I want to fight back for those lost and dying and going to hell. I want to fight back for the sake of our world. I want to fight back because the gospel moves me to do so. I want to fight back because "Complacency is a deadly foe of all spiritual growth,"[1] and I don't want to spiritually die. If we truly follow Jesus, we have no choice but to fight back.

I see the way we worship people, and I rise up, knowing my Bible tells me we were meant to worship only God.

I see the way the devil confuses us and takes us off course, and I rise up against his misuse of our reasonable desire to be loving, accepting, and open-minded to water down our standards.

I see the way we war against each other—in the Church, in our different races, in this world—and I rise up against that scheme of Satan's to divide us. I rise up and call it the sin it is.

It's time to make some heart determinations and declarations, my friends—to rise up, call out, stand firm, and walk strong. This is the time to rise up in holy anger, as Jesus did when He overturned the tables—to fight for holiness and purity and love. It's time to fight for the freedom from the devil's lies, which is ruining lives. It's time to fight for the truth to be revealed about who Jesus is and how only He has the power to save so that other powerless gods will no longer be put beside or before Him. It's time to fight for eyes to be opened about seemingly harmless distractions like social media and busy calendars and God-ish Christianity and how all of it at the end of the day keeps us from holiness. It's time to fight for us to truly revere and honor God again. We've lost that, I think, that healthy fear of God. We don't tremble before God anymore. We flaunt our independence.

There will be an element of holy anger in every decision to rise up. We often miss this because holy anger is not something we know— we know *flesh* anger, and that's different. Flesh anger is a reaction to things done against us; Holy anger is a response to things done against God. Jesus modeled righteous, holy anger in John 2, and when He did, it resulted in this prophetic word: "Passion for your house has consumed me, and the insults of those who insult you have fallen on me" (Psalm 69:9).

*Holy anger* should come naturally to a follower of Jesus Christ. It is the fierce defense that stems from our love for Him. If it's not present for an issue that moves God's heart, it is a good sign of a breakdown in that relationship. We should want what He wants, fight for what He fights for, honor what He honors in our everyday life, not just at a justice conference where we get stirred by a powerful speaker. This God-based passion leads regular, everyday people to put on warrior boots, rise up, and stand in what they believe.

If you've ever seen a person truly on fire for God, living with a noticeable passion, you must know that it is the outflow of a heart that has experienced the transformative power of Christ's presence. It goes beyond what a naturally born bold personality can do, because even those with zeal, energy, and drive run out at some point unless something bigger inside propels them forward. It's not something that can be put on; it is the reality of a changed soul who cannot help but see the world differently. When we are is face-to-face with the reality of how desperately we've veered from God's original design and plan, there is a natural anger that follows. It is driven by the understanding that this is not how things are supposed to be and the knowledge that what can truly change us is the Jesus we diminish and avoid.

*Flesh anger* is our reaction to personal injustices (things done to and against us) and trauma. (It's not that holy anger can never stem from this, but not usually.) We have the flesh anger down pat—road rage, verbal bashing, getting even, physical violence—*reaction, reaction, reaction to what you did to me*. But we are curiously passive when it comes to holy anger. We've cooked dinner every night and forgotten to weep angry tears for the soul-hungry foster kids whose parents have orphaned them in exchange for addiction. We've sat in carpool lines and forgotten to pray fiercely for our schools. We've gone to work and forgotten to tell our coworkers about Christ, forgetting that unless someone tells them, they are going to hell.

Where are the offended for the gospel? Where are the fighters for our kids? Where *am I*? These are tough love questions for us all. This is the time to throw off our weak and become strong. We may not want to hear it, but we must get real. Let us not think that we can afford any longer to coast and skate. There are real and present dangers, lives at risk, when we deny our need to rise up. If we love Jesus, there is no choice.

*We don't tremble before God anymore.*
*We flaunt our independence.*

**When we don't rise up, we toss away our influence.** We have the greatest news on the planet, know the One who can help us through the mess—we have everything other people don't even know they need. In *Secrets of the Secret Place*, Bob Sorge writes, "Those who make decisions based upon external data become thermometers of society...those who make their decisions based upon what they see in God become thermostats of society."[2] We should be setting the climate of the world, not adjusting to it. We should influence culture, not have culture influence us. We should be rising up and influencing the loudest because we come from a place of confidence, not arrogance, in the commitment we hold.

**When we don't rise up, we allow secular systems to make the rules.** We are kept silent by our insecurity, our fear, and our apathy.

We believe that we can't make a difference, that we don't have the right to say no and defend the true, biblical way. And all the while, systems are put in place and governments are shaped by our silence. We cannot blame a crazy world on others. We haven't risen up, and this is the result.

**When we don't rise up, we lie down and let Satan loose.** He never wins the ultimate war because we know for sure Jesus has that Winner title, forever. We are covered under that authority. But daily battles are being fought, and in them Satan still has a hand. (See 1 John, 1 Peter 5, and the story of Job for more.) We choose to either let him roam or pen him in his cage and shut him down by our offensive assertiveness for the gospel.

Not rising up has dire consequences. Let us not think that when we do not rise we preserve our safe, perfectly constructed life. It's not true. We are in a battle with evil whether or not we choose to engage with it. Satan is counting on us to be relaxed enough that we coast while he amps up his schemes, and in many cases, he's not been disappointed.

*We should want what God wants, fight for what He fights for, honor what He honors,*

So let us not fall for this. Let us, those in warrior boots, rise from our couches and go preach the gospel, for real. Let us rise from our desire to cocoon our families and from worry only about our preservation, misunderstanding totally our reason to be here on earth.[3]

Rise from our comfort. Rise from our silence. Rise from our indifference and desire to be popular and accepted. Rise for these kids. Rise for our future. Rise for the sake of the gospel and the love for our Jesus, which is the greatest compeller of all.

---

*Be sure to put your feet*
*in the right place, then stand firm.*
**ABRAHAM LINCOLN**

---

## Standing Firm

Most of our fear of rising and standing comes from our perception about what will happen if we do.

My friend Teri is watering her geraniums, and as she does, she notices a nest constructed in one of the pots, holding tiny robin's eggs. She leaves the nest undisturbed, but walks into her house and tells her husband.

"Be careful," he says. "You know snakes like to get in places like that to get the eggs." It is all Teri needs to make her decision. She goes back outside and swiftly disposes of the nest and eggs. And that is that.

That is, until the next morning when the Lord awakens her to remind her of the incident and speak to her heart. *Teri, at the threat of the enemy, you killed the opportunity for new life.* And she knows it is not about the eggs or the nest or the snake. It is about the bigger picture, of the Church, which, in its fearful state of the great what-ifs, rushes to remove anything that scares us. People who don't look like us or know the Christian language—people who have a rough background we can't relate to and get past—are swiftly marginalized and pushed away while we wind up keeping to our own kind, circling and serving each other in a small spiritual huddle. When all the while, God wants to use those unlike us to fortify weak places inside, sinful heart prejudice places within. We kill the opportunity to grow by ridding ourselves of the seeming threat of the unfamiliar. We remove our God-given opportunities for Kingdom service, though we long so deeply to serve God. But because the package doesn't look like we expected or the what-if list becomes long, we throw the opportunity away. And then we spend our life lamenting why God never uses us.

Fear drives the great majority of our life. It's why we don't witness. It's why we don't serve in ways that seem too risky or hard. (We'll go on short-term mission trips over spring break and take selfies with orphans, but to local jail ministry or ministry to the elderly we say no.) It's why we don't tell people hard truth or set healthy relationship boundaries. It's why some churches make rash and unloving decisions to cover up the sins of leadership or push those who don't appear to have full buy-in away. It's why we don't get vocal for the gospel. We are willing to kill beautiful things, beautiful potential, in order to make ourselves feel safer. And yet it's a smokescreen. We are no less at risk in this world when we passively wear our faith. We are just in an ineffective stance, wearing our flimsy flip-flops, unaware and unready, warrior boots not on and laced.

And let us not mistakenly think that when we live this way, reactive and killing good things out of fear, we will find a great burst of courage in a moment where our faith requires we be bold. There will be no cram course for this, no shortcut offered. We need to prepare now, not wing it when the time comes. Ephesians 6:10-18 puts it bluntly:

> Be strong in the Lord and in his mighty power. Put on all of God's armor so that you will be able to stand firm against all strategies of the devil. For we are not fighting flesh-and-blood enemies, but against evil rulers and authorities of the unseen world, against mighty powers in this dark world, and against evil spirits in the heavenly places.
>
> Therefore, put on every piece of God's armor so you will be able to resist the enemy in the time of evil. Then after the battle you will still be standing firm. Stand your ground, putting on the belt of truth and the body armor of God's righteousness. For shoes, put on the peace that comes from the Good News so that you will be fully prepared. In addition to all of these, hold up the shield of

faith to stop the fiery arrows of the devil. Put on salvation as your helmet, and take the sword of the Spirit, which is the word of God.

Pray in the Spirit at all times and on every occasion. Stay alert and be persistent in your prayers for all believers everywhere.

This is not a *when the time* comes conversation; it is a *before the time comes* list of what to do. This is a readiness call. God's call is a call of preparation. Jesus implores us to take an offensive stance, not a defensive one. We think that we can wait on further signs that we need to get serious about our spiritual lives. But are we really waiting on the world to prove to us how much crazier it can get? What further proof do we need than what has already been laid out for us in this passage and all throughout the Bible and in the tangibles we see every day? God tells us Satan has strategies. (Most of us at this point are familiar with his tricks.) He tells us we will have to fight for our lives. He tells us there is wicked out to get us, we will have fiery arrows coming our way, and we must stay awake and alert. Why, then, would we need to wait to hear one more headline story of bad news to take our lives seriously?

We are foolish to think that the way we live our lives daily does not matter. We are naive to believe that what we do right now does not determine how we are able to stand in the face of much tougher adversity. We practice and practice and practice some more. In this discipline, we become strong.

> *God's call is a call of preparation. Jesus implores us to take an offensive stance, not a defensive one.*

I am moved by a picture I see not long ago that goes around on social media—of 21 Coptic Christian martyrs in orange jumpsuits on bended knee at the lapping cusp of a beach in Libya. I know of the persecuted Church and know this is not new, but we in air-conditioned America haven't really seen the pictures much. To see real, live Jesus followers in their warrior boots in the flesh does something powerful to my spirit and frightens me to death, all at the same time. *This is what it looks like, isn't it, Jesus?* I ask Him, but I already in my heart know: it is how it is meant to end, not always or even usually with knives to the throat, but with Jesus being the Only Thing.

I grieve for my believing brothers, but at the same time, I envy their resolve. I want to look away from this picture because it makes me uncomfortable, and I know it is not the picture itself, but the commitment that is behind it. But I find myself looking closer, trying to see the faces to study them, believing in them I will see something, find something that shows me how to be a warrior too.

*What do these men have that I do not, that they can choose God like this? Were they born warriors? Were they fed special Jesus juice that they don't sell in my grocery store?* I ask in my mind, to no one in particular. As big as I can humanly think, as I cry and wonder, in my heart I believe I know. These men didn't just wake up one day ready to become martyrs. They didn't drink some special Jesus juice only found in their local markets, and they weren't just born innately strong. They were normal people made of flesh, born of birth canals, who had digestive systems and hands with knuckled fingers to pick up things they dropped on the floor and bad morning breath and hair that desperately needed combing after a restless night's sleep. They had loved ones who may not have loved God the same (though we know that many of them did), probably some really sweet mommas who begged them not to be so dedicated to their faith that over it they could lose their life, because that's just what most mommas would do.

These men were flesh-and-blood real. But when they came to the edge of the water that day, they came prepared. When they went down on their knees, their heart was already there. Their warrior boots were already on, and they were resolved and settled in what they would do, not feeling a surge of bravery; for no one made of flesh ever just becomes ready to die for the cause of Christ, though in that moment He has promised to make us strong. (Even Christ Himself asked that if there was another way than for Him to die that God would allow it—Matthew 26:39.) Martyrdom is something a life of choosing Him, over and over again, prepares us to be willing to do. In this way, we are all to live with the preparation to be martyrs, because we love Jesus that much and follow Him to the end, no matter what that looks like, which none of us know.

Were these men scared? I don't know, but I think: absolutely, yes, because this is the way of the flesh, even the best flesh among us. Will we be scared to choose God, whether it is a choice over our own daily comfort, the letting go of something we have learned to depend on that even feels easy, compared to this? Yes to this too. But even in their fear, were these men peaceful? I suspect this is a yes as well. To learn to surrender, we must learn to bow in the easier things. Otherwise we will never be ready to bow for real. And no matter how hard the bowing, Jesus, the Great Finisher of our lives, will be present with His Spirit in those hardest moments. This I do believe.

My friends, we have this same Spirit of God within us as these martyred brothers, making us into the warriors we never thought we could be. We don't bring on martyrdom or hardship in our life the more we surrender—we ready ourselves for any and every situation only God can foresee. We will never just one day wake up warriors. We will prepare for the day we need to become one and find out we already are.

This is why getting right before God today, and not waiting until tomorrow, is so vitally important. This is why we need to talk about hard things without changing the subject. (The hard things don't change with a changing subject.) This is why the search in the bottom of a bottle must end. This is why no more playing around with sex. This is why our marriages need to get right. This is why we have to stop playing church. This is why we can't just do whatever we want. This is why we need to be committed to holy living, at all costs—because sin kills the fight out of us and we need all the fight we can get. This is why the strength to stand has to be created in our hearts, now. This is why the urgent rally call to put our warrior boots on: our call to a life prepared.

Watchman Nee, the martyred believer I mentioned before, knew something of this. He was imprisoned for preaching the gospel in China, dying there while clinging to his deep and unwavering faith, like so many martyrs prior and since. He writes this part in *Sit, Walk, Stand*:

> No work is worthy to be called a work of God if God is not, in this sense, committing himself to it. It is the authorization to use his name that counts. We must be able to stand up and speak in his name. If not, our work lacks spiritual impact. But let me tell you, this is not something that can be "worked up" at a time of crisis. It is a fruit of obedience to God and of a resulting spiritual position known and maintained. It is something we must have already if it is to be available in a time of need.[4]

*Something we must already have. Known and maintained. Can't be worked up at a time of crisis.* Nee knew and stood for the truth. So did those 21 martyrs on the beach. Standing is training to learn how to stand; practice to get used to it. Standing is dozens of different moments of yes to God and no to self. It is the discipline of prayer and reading God's Word. It is not staying stuck in a repeat sin but coming to God in a posture of repentance and a contrite heart in full disclosure. We can't expect to stand for God without practicing. Otherwise, when the time comes, we will have no point of reference as to what to do.

And I know, we cannot practice everything. We cannot fully prepare ourselves enough to die for Christ, as that kind of faith and commitment eludes our human minds. But the daily practice of dying to ourselves, prayer, reading the Bible, serving others…is the practice field God has given us to use to help the hard moments not be so hard. We aren't born into becoming those people who become faith heroes. We take the practice field every day until it's time for the big game. None of us know when that big game will be or what it will look like.

And in this stance, we must be fully dedicated to the understanding that the world will not like our position, so the great wisdom of Jesus is required to maneuver potentially volatile waters. I cannot emphasize this enough. Before we speak, we need His wisdom. Before we share our standard or position on an issue, we must ask Him to guard our tongues with love, to help us know when to speak and when not to. Many people have been turned off by the approach of a Jesus follower not led by the Spirit. It is reckless and sinful to jump ahead of God and be moved by our personal preferences, annoyances, and assumptions, and it never works in representing God well. We must begin to see how our behavior has turned people off, mourn it, confess it, and ask God to help us live the gospel differently. We have to become so in tune with God that even if someone is mad at our position and vehemently disagrees, they respect our approach. This, my friends, is possible.

Although the world doesn't have the insight to know this about itself, it is looking for someone to place their feet firmly and take a stand. There's a reason there's so much party fighting around an election (my writing of this book just so happens to coincide with an especially contentious election year) and so much chaos when no one truly honest and strong steps up: it's looking for leadership, though it claims it wants to be left alone. It's just like back in Moses' day, when he goes on the mountain to be with God for 40 days and nights and the people he is leading that he leaves behind don't quite know what to do with themselves, though they are always fighting to do their own thing. Aaron, Moses' right hand, is left in charge, and all they want to know is where is the nearest god to lead them in Moses' place and if there isn't one, can they make one up?

Aaron caves and the golden god is made. God is angry, and but for the good favor of Moses would have taken them all out. Man wanting leadership and going about it the wrong way, just like today. People wanting direction in the midst of their wanderings. Same song, second verse.

All of us want someone to take a stand. We respect it, if just for the simple reason that so few ever do. If we will learn to love people with the heart of God while honoring our commitments to Him, we can stand in the right way and have a real opportunity to turn hearts toward Him. In our commitment to standard, there must always be the deeper desire to watch God save.

> *We must begin to see how our behavior has turned people off, mourn it, confess it, and ask God to help us live the gospel differently.*

And yes, standing up for God will mean learning to accept being in the minority, as lonely as that sounds. We who follow Jesus will need to determine we will stand up for Him even if we stand alone. Jesus was never a numbers guy. He had His close 12. He fed a large crowd with just five loaves and two fish. He says in Matthew 18:20, "Where two or three gather together as my followers, I am there among them." Throughout Scripture He reminds us of the faithful few, the remnant, who follow Him until the end (Judges 7; Isaiah 6:10; Jeremiah 4; Romans 9). A warrior boots believer won't spend their life looking over their shoulder for the numbers; they will worry only about being faithful themselves, to the end.

I remember a picture I once saw of a young man, kneeling at a metal flagpole outside of his school, head to the cold metal, with not one single other soul in sight. See You at the Pole Day for Jesus followers, a student-initiated and student-led movement, began in Texas in 1990 with a single church youth group and grew to more than 3 million by 1998. I remember the movement in its heyday. It was a powerful morning for so many students who exercised their right to stand up in public for God.

Though it's diminished some, in many places the movement is still going strong. But as the world gets harder and the minority grows smaller, the hard reality is there are few kids like this young man in the picture who will stand for God, alone. His courage and commitment bring tears to my soft momma heart. I know how hard it had to be for him, as a teenager who is at the height of his desire to be accepted, to walk up to that pole alone…kneel alone…pray alone. But God saw him out there that day. And hard as it may have been on earth, God will remember his faithfulness in heaven.

We come into this world alone and we will one day leave it alone. In that moment of our very last breath, it will be us and God—not our gathered followers, friends, or even family. It is the way He intended it when He created us. Our faith is singular, with the gift of God to give us community so we don't have to walk it out alone. Our community is beautiful, but we can't hide behind it—He still sees us as one. Despite our human desire not to be left alone, we don't need anyone else to stand with us when we stand up for God. In that moment, His is the only hand we need to hold.

Standing up for God is not charity work, nor should we think it is too much for a sacrificial move. Standing up for God will save our sanity, because in our commitment our mind has a place to anchor and rest. Standing up for God changes how we walk, how we make decisions, how steadfast and steady we are. We have settled on something and it alters our life. No longer do we wander. Standing up for God gives us a purpose—it leads other people to the saving knowledge of Jesus Christ. This alone helps our life make sense.

*We need to stand up for God
even if we stand alone.*

### Active Faith

A debit card won't work until you activate it.

I should know, since a couple of days ago some guy in another state tried to charge a couple of steep concert tickets to my account, to the tune of $750, and made me have to get a new one. Once again I am reminded of how inconvenience brings out my ugly, as I have whined and lamented on and on to people for days that this is something I have to do.

The card arrives with the sticker on the front that says to validate it and that I should do it on the spot, but I don't. Instead, I wait until I am in the grocery store line with five shoppers behind me, all with packed carts, all staring at me as I slink off to quickly call the 800 number to activate the card. Embarrassing as it is, it must be done. The card is useless until I activate it.

In the same way, rising and standing are the ways we activate the Word of God in our lives. Otherwise, we have a powerful tool we never do anything with. It's our initiative into the process of watching God make active the promises in His Word: to provide peace, to be enough, to give strength and wisdom, to complete the good work He's started in our lives…and so many other promises. It's our faith being set into motion by our purposeful activity on the front end. Without it, our faith is not active. It is something we talk about and think about and tell others about but never ourselves experience because we do not activate the power in our hands.

In his book *Walking with God*,[5] John Eldredge writes about how we make agreements with a negative thought that comes into our brain (hello, Satan) and before we know it we have spent years with destructive agreements running our life and living in our head. I must raise my hand to testify. I've made agreements with things that haven't been of God. Some of them haven't been good and have stuck with me for nearly a lifetime, especially ones about love.

But if I flip this idea around, when I think about the faith piece of our lives, I know that agreements can also be the very thing we need to walk Jesus strong, once and for all, when they are agreements made with God.

To agree that God is good no matter what is to activate our faith. To agree that He is in control and Sovereign is to say *yes and amen* to His character. To agree that He is the Savior of the world and the only way to heaven is to solidify our future, confirm in our hearts where we will one day go. The promises and character of God do not depend on whether or not we agree with them. They will come true and be true, no matter what. But as humans in our lives as we walk them out, how those promises and character manifest in our lives requires we come into agreement with them to activate their full power and potential in our life (1 John 5:14-15).

Making the warrior boots declaration *I will rise up and stand firm* is saying, *Yes, God, I will be active in my faith.* There's a reason faith, like a debit card, has to be activated—because it requires something of us—something only we, the cardholder, can do, and that's needed in our spiritual relationship. If Jesus wanted to skip that step, He would have. We activate His Word (make it come alive) in our life when we come into agreement with it (2 Corinthians 1:20). Without that piece on our part, we resign ourselves to a passive faith with all the potential wasted on our inactivity.

*Passive faith* says, "I'll wait on God to make every detail of my future clear and then I'll make a move." *Active faith* says, "I'll pray and walk in the prompting of God, no matter if it makes sense."

*Passive faith* says, "I'll sit and collect biblical information for years on end and stay satisfied with getting spiritually fat." *Active faith* says, "I will use my life to preach the gospel and serve others with the information I know now."

*Passive faith* says, "I'll settle for fear, doubt, and a reactionary life and hope not to be taken down by my struggle." *Active faith* says, "I will never settle for sin or living a life without true strength and joy and will, instead, do what it takes to make my relationship with God right and have a thriving life at all costs."

We take on the commitment to rising and standing so that we get used to the life of an active faith. Otherwise, we are ill-equipped to do any hard thing, fearful of everything God asks. When we live passively in our faith, we become like the Israelites in the day of Amos who had compromised so long they had gotten used to halfhearted living. "'My people have forgotten what it means to do right,' says the LORD" (Amos 3:10). The commentary in my New Living Translation Bible says it like this: "The people of Israel no longer knew how to do what was right. The more they sinned, the harder it was to remember what God wanted." A lot of us have let this go on too long. We've let ourselves slide spiritually. And now we don't even remember what God wants from us. We are fat on our spiritual knowledge and slim on our faith in action because all we know, really, is what we want ourselves.

The longer we live this ill-equipped way, the more we will fear the life of a spiritual warrior. (A sign that this, indeed, is us is how we react to the thought of exercising our faith.) It will be so foreign to us that we have no place for it in our minds. And the cycle will continue until finally we concede to a life of vapid nothing, or we grow so sick of being stale we do the hard, uphill things to get us out of it or life forces us to into that position. Only then, we are at the end. Then we have been plundered by the enemy, as was the fate of the Israelites in their forgetting-God state: "'Therefore,' says the Sovereign LORD, 'an enemy is coming! He will surround them and shatter their defenses. Then he will plunder all their fortresses'" (verse 11).

Waiting to activate our faith is a choice to let ourselves be ravaged by an enemy who counts on us being out of shape and caught off guard. We can't go our whole life not remembering what God wants, choosing what we want over Him—it's far too big of a risk.

The day is here. The battle is on. The enemy is present.

## Get Low (Before You Rise Up)

God is not typically chatty with me, even when He speaks to my heart. Most of the time it's a phrase or two, or even just a few words, and never things I would think up for myself, because they are usually things that make me uncomfortable. I think sometimes because authors tend to pack most of our *God speaking to me* stories into a book or books, we who read the books start to feel like there is some sort of constant chat line going on that we have missed out on getting the number. But it's not true, at least for me. God does speak to my heart, but because it's not every day and not all the time, when He does, I pay close attention.

*Get low*, He says to me not long ago, and I know it is His call to me for greater humility and prayer. When my flesh runs amuck, I can get such nasty pride and jealousy and feelings of entitlement. It's so egregious, it's hard to write. I want what other people have. I resent things that do not come my way. I feel I deserve them. This is the albatross of flesh I wear that makes me revolt from holiness in a way that makes me sick. And then sometimes I am gracious and humble and generous and know in my bones I am not entitled to a single thing, and I live in that contented space in my very best me skin, by the help of the Holy Spirit. These are the days and moments I do well.

But the only way those days exist are when I get low in prayer. The days I have courage are those days too. And the days I stare fear in the face and conquer it, live wisely, and preach the gospel without concern for ramification. The only days I am ever doing well are the days I have first gotten low in prayer. It's a myth to think we can do well and be strong without the supernatural power of prayer fueling the cause. A strong person first lowers her voice in prayer so God can raise her voice up in the world.

Rising up and standing firm will not happen without first getting low before God. Otherwise we will rise in our own ambition, stand in our own opinion, operate in our own flesh. We may get a moment of adrenaline and rise in it, but if we aren't low before God first, it will fizzle out. Getting low is the call of God for us to come to the power source to help us be the people we cannot be. I am not determined enough to rise against opposition. I'm not steady enough to stand firm. I need God to put me in those powerful positions. He will, if we just come to Him and ask.

The greatest risk to our declaration that we will rise up and stand firm is not in our lack of bravery but in letting our prayer life slide. That's the secret to power, not pep talks to ourselves. It is as author and minister S.D. Gordon said, "The greatest thing anyone can do for God and man is pray. It is not the only thing; but it is the chief thing. The great people of the earth today are the people who pray. I do not mean those who talk about prayer; nor those who say they believe in prayer; nor those who can explain about prayer; but I mean those people who take time to pray."[6] It's too hard out there; letting our prayer life slide is to the detriment of our survival.

*A strong person first lowers her voice in prayer so God can raise her voice up in the world.*

A few weeks ago, my family visits beautiful California for my son's graduation from high school. We spend nine glorious days in this gorgeous state, eating our weight in In and Out burgers, driving the Pacific Coast Highway, doing all kinds of fun family things. On the last day we find ourselves in La Jolla, California, one of the most breathtaking stops on our trip. The salty air calls to us, and before we know it, we find our family of five in kayaks, paddling the Pacific Ocean, being led by a tanned, knowledgeable guide. The sights and experiences are incredible.

"This is the house of Dr. Seuss," the guide says as we stop for a minute for his commentary, pointing back up to the shore. "And this one, the owners of *Vanity Fair.*" Our eyes cannot take in all the lavish homes they see, there are so many. Huge homes. Majestic. All built into the side of a mountain. He's telling us the backstory and why this house and that.

And then he points to the homes, mansions really, closest to the edge of the water, sloping downhill uncomfortably. He tells us about how these homes, once worth millions of dollars, are now almost uninhabitable, with warning signs on the front door about how one day they will likely fall into the ocean. And how as beautiful as they are, no one wants to live in them. The erosion of the land is simply too big a risk to take to invest such high dollars in, since one day they will all slide away.

Erosion is not just for fancy homes on the ocean. It's a reality of human life that can make other beautiful things go away too. *Erosion*: to eat into or away; destroy by slow consumption or disintegration. It's usually the slow death of things that take the good things from us.

I think of my marriage and how sometimes it begs for my attention and I push it down, push it away because I'm too busy to deal with it today. I think of my friendships I need to check on and nurture, but because I don't have the energy, I never pick up the phone. I think of my spiritual life and how it's been days since I've had a really good personal time with God and how I just keep saying I will do it tomorrow. And I know: all of these things won't die instantly (maybe knowing that is a problem). They will die slowly over time by means of erosion—not paying attention, not taking care of things when they need to be, believing doing it sometime soon is soon enough. One day I will wake up and the things I love and value will be gone. They will have disintegrated...slid into a sea of nothingness all because I didn't rise up and pay them enough attention.

And how will we fight this slippery slope in our spiritual lives? By our everyday, small but mighty rising ups, standing firms. By getting low. We make deposits into our lives, practice spiritual strength training every day. We build up our own stability. (By not doing so, we only hurt ourselves.) We reject erosion by these everyday choices and commitments so it never becomes our fate. We rise up and stand firm so erosion is not allowed to slide into our lives and slide us away. We live the words of Jesus in 1 Corinthians 16:13 for the rest of our lives: "Be on guard. Stand firm in the faith. Be courageous. Be strong."

And we remember most of all that it is always and only the power of God that gives us the courage to do anything. It will only be His power to help us walk Jesus strong. That if we rise up and if we stand firm it will only be because the love of our God compels us, and He alone sees our weakness through. For He will not ask us to do what He Himself will not. He was the God of David who *stood with* him when Saul was trying to kill him, able to testify these precious words: "In his unfailing love, my God will stand with me" (Psalm 59:10). He was the God of Jeremiah who *stood beside* him when rejected by the people and persecuted by Pashur for preaching the gospel—a message that God Himself put within his bones. Even in his lamenting, Jeremiah knew of the companionship of God despite suffering, the mighty source of his strength: "But the LORD stands beside me like a great warrior" (Jeremiah 20:11).

And with our trembling knees and human skin, this same God will stand with us.

# I WILL RISE UP AND STAND FIRM

**Take a Deeper Dive:** 1 John 5

**10 minutes:** Welcome. Share about a time you stood your ground about something (funny or serious).

**10 Minutes:** Intro to chapter through Video Teaching with Lisa (outline and videos available online at www.warriorbootsbook.com)

**35 Minutes:** Small Group Discussion (Take the first 10 minutes to answer privately, then the last 25 to discuss as a group.)

1. What do you think of this idea of rising up in righteous anger?

2. What is the biggest hindrance to believers rising up, and what is the greatest risk when we don't?

3. Reread Ephesians 6:10-18. Why is this passage vital in the context of standing firm?

4. Discuss the active faith versus passive faith section— which of these active versus passive relate the most to you?

5. What does the "getting low" life look like? Share the benefits of a rich and thriving prayer life, especially in these tough times.

**Prayer:** God, help us rise up—against injustice, our own sin, for the Kingdom and the gospel. Help us stand firm and strong in what we believe. May we know the difference between our flesh anger and the righteous anger You ask us to have over things that break Your heart. Help us to be active in our faith and no longer passive. We get low before You today and say You are God. Yes and amen.

**Bonus Home Helps:**

1. Do a word study of *stand* from Scripture.

2. Memorize and meditate on Psalm 20:8: "But we will rise up and stand firm." (Substitute the word *I* for *we* to personalize it.)

3. Pick a different person per day for five days who needs you to fight for them in prayer and pray specifically with a battle mentality and passion.

4. Pick one of the three "active faith" characteristics and this week do something tangible in your life to support and pursue it.

5. Ask someone close to you to pray for you to have the strength to rise up and stand firm in what you believe and live out this seven-word (*I Will Rise Up and Stand Firm*) declaration in your life.

# I WILL GO ON RECORD

*When Christ calls a man,*
*He bids him come and die.*
**DIETRICH BONHOEFFER**

I wonder if Stephen, "a man full of God's grace and power" (Acts 6:8), ever woke up in a fearful cold sweat. This happens to me sometimes when I wake to the reality of what I'm up against in this world and it overwhelms me, and I need to believe it happened to my heroes of the faith too. I suspect Satan prowls and pounces greater in the night when it's silent and dark—when the TV has been shut off and the phone has been powered down. It's when he tries to get to me, I know.

In one way I know for sure Stephen is like you and me: he was up against some stuff in his world. He comes on the scene in Acts 6, when the early church is experiencing its first official growing pains—complaints of not being fairly treated among members, some not getting enough food (in those days sharing food and homes was a necessity), favoritism, human beings wearing flesh and not getting along. It's all so scary familiar. Lest we think the early church was perfect, we need only remember that even back then, it was made up of people. As we know, people will ruin a perfect thing, every single time.

Stephen becomes one of the seven men chosen to help solve this food delegation problem. Though all the men chosen are clearly faithful and godly men, Stephen is the only one in the Bible with such a tagline after his name: "a man full of faith and the Holy Spirit" (verse 5). Within a few verses, he's called out twice with taglines for being amazing, so he obviously is.

Stephen's also quite vocal—I'm guessing the most vocal of the seven since he is the one who gets in the debates with some of the Jewish men and as a result becomes the one who ticks them off. Powerful in word and deed, this man named Stephen. Starts in places of service, gets moved to a position of authority, and becomes a powerful mouthpiece for God, a lauded example of a person going on record for his faith. He gets attention, but it's not for being popular.

Stephen is strong in his faith. Without a doubt, he has his warrior boots on while he lives and when he dies. His life wasn't just about being a martyr—I think sometimes we have only this impression with images in our minds of the brutal, unspeakable stoning scene at the close of Acts 7:

> Then they put their hands over their ears and began shouting. They rushed at him and dragged him out of the city and began to stone him...
>
> As they stoned him, Stephen prayed, "Lord Jesus, receive my spirit." He fell to his knees, shouting, "Lord, don't charge them with this sin!" And with that, he died (verses 57-60).

No, Stephen was much more than his death—he was a human being who grew into this place but was a fierce God-lover from the start. He loved God when he was in a service position. He loved God still when the Lord moved him up. This is how it happens with God's anointing and appointing: those in warrior boots are faithful in all places. Only when we get sidetracked and focus on self do we love God more when He gives us something to do that is big.

The reality of Stephen's life is Jesus, Jesus, Jesus and how he is compelled to go on record for his faith, no matter what this means.

We don't want to think about such devotion, for we know ours may not stand up. Stephen preaches *anyway*. I think it is the way we need to learn to preach in this day and time when preaching is only popular if culture accepts it. Conviction messages aren't our favorite. The world shies away. And yet Jesus is worth it. We tell Him that so easily, but when we live and preach *anyway* is when it truly shows.

Samuel Brengle, a founding leader in the Salvation Army, said it like this:

> After you have taken the step of faith, you must talk your faith. Those who are not afraid to announce their convictions to the world and defend them will have true stability. It is so in politics, in business, in all moral reforms, and in salvation. A universal law underlies the declaration, "with the mouth confession is made unto salvation" (Romans 10:10 KJV). If you would remain sanctified, you must put yourself on record before the devils in hell, your acquaintances on earth, and the angels in heaven. You must stand before the world professing and possessing heart purity. Only in this way can you burn the bridges behind you. Until all are destroyed, you are not safe.[1]

*True stability. Until all are destroyed, you are not safe.* We don't think of going on record as having these benefits—all we know is that we are scared because of how it may turn out. We fear that if we speak up for God, put ourselves on record for what we believe, it may not go well. We think to ourselves that if we don't speak it officially, we can go on with our safe suburban life, driving our freshly washed Honda, and loving God quietly while the world leaves us alone. We don't factor in that the abandon for the cross is what rescues us from fear because internally it fortifies us in a way no outside scary thing can take away. The more we speak up and speak out for God, the more we become strong in Him.

These are the things Stephen knew and lived. These are the things we must know and live too, as we are up against this crazy world.

Going on record is the signature on the contract that has already been drawn up. It's really just the next step in our faith—the sealing of our decision to rise up and stand firm in our warrior boots of strength. We can't truly be with God if we aren't willing to identify with Him. If we stay silent about the One we love, this is not a relationship based on commitment; it is a relationship built on convenience. To only want to be connected with God when it doesn't cost us anything should keep us awake at night over how we can change, shake us to our core because it is a gospel according to ourselves. We will never be spiritually stable when we aren't willing to vocally affirm our decision to follow Christ.

I know we are scared. I know, when we silence the phone and don't deflect and force our mind to other things, we wake up in the night in cold sweats, fearing what a vocal faith may do to us. I know we imagine hard days and wonder if we are strong enough in the faith to endure them. But we can't pretend anymore that staying silent about our faith will get us through—that it doesn't disable us for the future when the world makes us speak up for or against God, in one way or another. The truth is, in some ways, when we do the work of rising up and standing firm, going on record for God is the natural next step.

I also know that sometimes, in order to sincerely resist the infighting of the Church and the hot-button culture conflict—in our claims not to want to be known as a person *against* something, but rather *for* something—we unwittingly leave Jesus hanging. Yes, the road narrows when we go on record for our faith. No, not everyone will like it, and some, in order to jab below the belt, will call it judgmental and fighting *against*. But with the heart intent to be *for God*, it is the right and only choice to make. And we have to be strong enough to weather the unwarranted accusation and live our truth.

The bottom line is, friends, that if we're honest with ourselves we will admit some hard things: that we have settled into the fact that we are counting on others to be more vocal, to step up as the Jesus mouthpiece on behalf of us, and under that assertion, we run away from the burden and responsibility. That we rise and fall with the news that worries us, forgetting totally about the strength and power of God as His children we, too, possess. We have become like the people led by Joshua in Joshua 7 who after God had helped conquer difficult tasks got defeated and became "paralyzed with fear at this turn of events, and their courage melted away" (verse 5). Some of us felt strong at one time and now we don't. Some of us have wanted to be vocal for God but our fear has silenced us. We can't change the ways we've failed to exercise a strong faith in the past, but by the grace of God we can move forward and do it differently.

Catherine of Siena once said, "Proclaim the truth and do not be silent through fear." It's what Stephen lived. It's what we can live too.

> *If we stay silent about the One we love, this is not a relationship based on commitment; it is a relationship built on convenience.*

### Fierce Love

Recently God is calling me out—calling me to love Him more fiercely and exhort others to love Him fiercely too. See, sisters and brothers of the faith, we are all in this together. We are all in the same human boat, held back by our flesh, wanting to want God more but being afraid to take the faith walk with Him in our everyday life. I want to love God fiercely. I want to get off the fence of embarrassment and desiring to be loved and thought of as mainstream instead of a Jesus freak and abandon myself to life on the other side—the life of Jesus, Jesus, Jesus, like Stephen.

God deserves a fierce love. He calls us to it. We have to come to the point in our lives where we decide to love God fiercely or not at all. Everything flows from this choice. This is what He requires of us, though we still often tell ourselves that an adequate faith will do. There is a reason people at the end of their lives often get more serious about God—people who have waffled before and wandered and lived halfhearted in their convictions—because they know that now they are about to see Him for real, and as they kneel before Him, what will they say? That they thought going to church was enough? That they thought because they lived cleaner than a lot of other people He would say well done? It's not that God is so picky and judgmental with us that He is up there somewhere, counting up our hours of community service and time we spend in the Word. There is no need for Him to do that. Our activity down here speaks for itself. Our bond with God is one we cannot make up—either we are or aren't close with Him. God knows if our love for Him is fierce or it isn't. No smokescreens, no spin, no manufacturing. It shows.

We shouldn't have to know what a fierce love will require—we either say yes or no to loving Jesus hard and walk out that decision. A fierce love for God doesn't make excuses. How fiercely we love God will determine how willing we will be to go on record, how committed we are to warrior boots living. It will take a fierce love of God, all we have to give, to protect His Word and His place in our lives…to point all the attention to Him when given a platform…to honor His unmatched gift of death on the cross. If we've never been able to really stand for these things before, our love is not fierce. And lest we question…it doesn't take a loud or bold personality type to love God fierce. Personality is irrelevant. My mother is one of the most soft-spoken, meek women I know, but she has a bulldog love for God. I've watched this naturally shy woman walk straight up to strangers and tell them about her Jesus on many occasions in my life, like a flaming arrow from a bow. It doesn't take loud and bold. It takes fierce and love.

A fierce love for God will not allow others to diminish our Savior. It will become offended when the world tries to claim He is not enough. A fierce love will not let anyone take the praise that goes to

Him. It will never give the excuse that it doesn't need to rise or rally in the face of an injustice that breaks the heart of God. A fierce love won't be an occasional burst of bravery but the way we live our daily life or the ink betrays me.

A fierce love requires our own faith to be taken seriously, without excuse for ourselves…a going on record of holy living…a tenacious defense of Jesus Christ, our Lord.

It will always come down to how fiercely we love Him.

> *A fierce love won't be an occasional burst of bravery but the way we live our daily life.*

## Fierce Loyalty

It's interesting, what tattoos have secretly made many Jesus followers do. Some of us didn't even mean to, as we followed the culture trends, but we've gone on record already with our verses tattooed on our wrists, Christian fish on our shoulder, Jesus pictures on our skin. Did we count the cost of this when we were willfully tattooed? For some of us, I think not. The reality of this going on record is that one day, maybe sooner than we think, we will have to stand by what we display. We better do the work now to prepare for that.

Even now, I think of how I've branded myself to Jesus every time I hand my money to the drive-thru employee at the Starbucks or McDonald's or wherever I am. I see them glance down at my wrist and the *Romans 1:16* staring back at them. And I know I cannot afford to be my normal Lisa flesh at this moment, no matter how I feel or how bad they messed up the order…because I have now brought Jesus into it and what they think of Him rides on me. Some days, the bad ones, it is an especially sobering thought. The truth is, I can wear my fierce loyalty to Jesus on my wrist, but I better have this fierce loyalty to Him in my life or the ink betrays me.

Long before tattoos, Jesus valued fierce loyalty to Him even at the late hour of the cross. It was the vocal affirmation of Him by a convicted criminal as they were being crucified that resulted in the saving of his life—a going on record to ask to be associated with the Lord, from the most unlikely source, which was heard by God and rewarded.

> Two others, both criminals, were led out to be executed with him. When they came to a place called The Skull, they nailed him to the cross. And the criminals were also crucified—one on his right and one on his left.
>
> Jesus said, "Father, forgive them, for they don't know what they are doing." And the soldiers gambled for his clothes by throwing dice.
>
> The crowd watched and the leaders scoffed. "He saved others," they said, "let him save himself if he is really God's Messiah, the Chosen One." The soldiers mocked him too, by offering him a drink of sour wine. They called out to him, "If you are the King of the Jews, save yourself!" A sign was fastened above him with these words: "This is the King of the Jews."
>
> One of the criminals hanging beside him scoffed, "So you're the Messiah, are you? Prove it by saving yourself— and us too, while you're at it!"
>
> But the other criminal protested, "Don't you fear God even when you have been sentenced to die? We deserve to die for our crimes, but this man hasn't done anything wrong." Then he said, "Jesus, remember me when you come into your Kingdom."
>
> And Jesus replied, "I assure you, today you will be with me in paradise" (Luke 23:32-43).

It is not enough that we sit in our churches and sing worship songs. It is not enough to tweet verses and spiritual sayings and go to conferences and Bible studies. Our loyalty for God must be fierce, in our neighborhoods, on the ball field, on vacation in a tropical place where no one knows where we've come from. It matters not to God that we can sit with other believers and profess Him, though He has ordained for us to do so for the sake of fellowship and strengthening of the body (Acts 2). But our loyalty to God must surpass the Christian camp moments. We have to go on record for Him in the everyday of our lives, no matter the audience.

*A fierce loyalty to God* will fiercely protect His Word, His divinity, and the Spirit inside of us that can grieve and be breached when we reject His promptings and cave in to sin (Ephesians 4:14-32).

*A fierce loyalty to God* will fiercely honor the holiness and power of God, His kindness and grace and, yes, jealousy, and never take those things for granted or minimize their importance.

*A fierce loyalty to God* will fiercely serve God and people. Not just when we feel like it or it serves us. Serving, always. A heart of service. An attitude of service. When we serve God, we want to serve people. They naturally go together.

*A fierce loyalty to God* will fiercely stay with Him—forgo the way of fickle spiritual living.

Living fiercely loyal to God clears out so much complication because in a moment of weakness, we do not have to choose. Like the other issues that we have talked about in this book, we have resolved complications for ourselves in advance. We have made up our mind and gone on record, and in that space, people know who we are and know what we believe. No scrambling needed. God is our God is our God, and we live according to what His Word says. Other people know to expect it. We have committed ourselves to a lifestyle we can't and won't back our way out of, so nothing has to be figured out on the fly. There is something empowering about having already made a choice for God and simply living that choice out. It makes life much less complicated. It is the reason behind the importance of making declarations over our life—so that in choosing up front we have put the rest of our life in order. And in that order, there is strength. Outside chaos doesn't affect a life of choice and conviction like it does a life without definitives.

When we live fiercely loyal to God, we will say the hard, unpopular things because our loyalty to God supersedes our need to be liked. We won't want to dishonor God or diminish His place in our lives. This is why it's so important we remember God and dwell on the things He has done for us—fight to recall such things in our everyday lives when it is our tendency to forget: because when we remember God and all He has done for us our heart swells with love and loyalty. This is our God. We would die before we would deny or dishonor Him. It's only when we forget His Kingship and begin to treat Him casually that our attitude toward Him begins to slide and we go into a mode of self-promotion and preservation at all costs. (We can't be fiercely loyal to self and God at the same time.)

When we live fiercely loyal to God, we have the strength to walk warrior boots strong—to rise from our everyday, normal life and be people we never thought we could be, not out of our great talent, but out of the powerful Spirit inside. God can use our tattoos to tell of His greatness and worthiness for us to identify with Him because God can use anything. But He doesn't need them. And He also wants to use the everyday evidence of a life that looks like Jesus, one that is undeniably linked to Him…no skin ink necessary.

*Living fiercely loyal to God clears out so much complication because in a moment of weakness, we do not have to choose.*

## Going on Record

Stand up for me against world opinion and I'll stand up for you before my Father in heaven…If you don't go all the way with me, through thick and thin, you don't deserve me. If your first concern is to look after yourself, you'll never find yourself. But if you forget about yourself and look to me, you'll find both yourself and me" (Matthew 10:32,38-39 MSG).

Going on record as a follower of Jesus isn't to be taken casually. People have lost their lives over this allegiance to God. This should sober us but not frighten us. It should move us to ready ourselves, that we might also be Jesus strong in the face of uncertainty and, God forbid, death. The truth is, none of us know how this whole thing will turn out for us because we do not know the future. The only certain thing is Jesus and no matter what, as a believer in Him, the knowledge for us that in the end we will be okay.

I thank God for the people who have gone on record. I long to learn from their fortitude and courage. The young Rachel Scott in the schoolyard at Columbine with a gun to the head who when asked, "Do you still believe in God?" replied to her killer, "You know I do" and went to be with Him in the next minute as the killer pulled the trigger. People like Kayla Mueller, the American hostage who was tortured, forced into slave labor by ISIS, and eventually killed, who stood up to her executioner to deny her abandonment from her Christian faith. Bible heroes like John the Baptist, who was brutally beheaded under orders from Herod for his outspoken and unwavering faith. The young Rachel Scotts and Kayla Muellers of the world teach me—give me hope that in my flesh, true strength can be mine, evidence that Jesus inside is enough for literally anything. These young women were strong, but they were human. John the Baptist was too. All of them lost their life after going on record for their faith. They died, yes, but they died fully alive in Him. The final word was not death in these lives; it was *Jesus*.

No matter what—no matter the fear or the insecurity or the not knowing how it will all turn out—our life must be a record that we walk with Him. We must emulate Him in every way, and we must tell others how and why He is the reason for our life. We cannot keep quiet about Jesus, no matter if it is a quiet or reserved personality we have. God can compensate for those timid places inside of us. If our God can part the Red Sea, can He not cause a feeble mouth to testify to His goodness?

The biggest factors that will help us speak up for Him will be how fiercely we love Him, if we have truly died to self (a daily, recurring death, by the way), and how urgently we believe the gospel is necessary. My word, do we really need more proof that the world is dying and in desperate need of an alternative for the way we've lived? It's urgent, friends. It's dire. The house is not just near a flame, it is fully on fire. We don't need another shooting to tell us our hearts are at war. We don't need more terrorism to tell us we are at risk. We, as believers, are being called out for such a time as this to raise our voices and lead people to the Truth and the Way. Not tomorrow. *Now*.

We are called out to be the Esther in this moment, the representation, the mouthpiece, the risker for the lives of many. Esther, the Jewish beauty who has become queen, with the Spirit of God inside that makes her Jesus strong. How else can she approach the king to ask him to save her people, the ones his prime minister and second in command, Haman, has ordered killed because of his pride and hatred (Esther 3)? This is too big of a risk. A momentary brave won't cut it. It's too big of a job for one woman, queen or not. But she is compelled to choose life. She is compelled to choose good at any cost. This is the choice of every believer at some point: truth and good over self-preservation and fear.

Esther is implored by her righteous love for God and people, spurred on by the words of her cousin Mordecai, who reminds her of what is at risk if she chooses silence: "If you keep quiet at a time like this, deliverance for the Jews will arise from some other place, but you and your relatives will die. What's more, who can say but that you have been elevated to the palace for just such a time as this?" (4:14). He is reminding her that God will be faithful, no matter what. God will deliver His people, as He's promised. He's always going to do His thing. But in that plan, He wants to use her to accomplish such powerful good. She can be a part of it or not. It has to take precedence over feelings for her to move forward. It has to supersede the consequence of risk for her to become involved.

God empowered Esther, but He still gave her a choice—to rely on His power and strength to do an amazing thing or choose to sit quietly, ruled by fear. God gives us this choice too. He's gifted us, every one. He has jobs for us. But He lets us choose whether or not to take them on. Our struggle in life is when we take the easier, safer road, which may provide relief in the moment, but in the end leaves us feeling lost and unfulfilled in our destiny. This conflicted life, many of us know well.

God will be God, with or without us. He will become known and worshipped by all, the Bible says (Romans 14:10; Psalm 72:11). But we have been appointed to speak up now. God wants to use us, each of us, for such a time as this to lead others to a saving relationship with Him. The irony of this is that while it may seem a sacrifice, it is the thing that will save our lives too. To go through life with a rock-solid core that fear and insecurity cannot throw off is the best strategy. This is the deep desire of us all—we spend our lives trying to figure out how to become less fearful and more secure, and when pep talks don't do it, some of us finally turn to prayer. When we have tried all the skin care, exercised all the many days, bought all the many things, drank all the liquid courage in the bottle, made all the money that was supposed to help us, we sit with all our insecurity still very much intact because none of it ever helps us, long term. Only our life being used for God brings lasting things. Only serving God with His holy courage burning inside changes us into less fearful people. We won't brave ourselves into it in a shining moment. We will only have what it takes when we spend our life going on record for Jesus. Then and only then will it become the natural response, despite the risk or size of the task.

It's time, yes. Time to go on record. Time to live our place in God's plan, like Esther. It's time, too, to live a different strategy than defensively scared. It's time, instead, to ready our lives by daily, faithfully going on record so people know what to expect from us and we put ourselves in a position that we can't back out of in fear.

It's time to make Romans 1:16 our rally cry, "For I am not ashamed of the gospel of Christ" (NKJV), knowing that it truly is the "power to save all who believe" (GNT). You. Me. Us. That neighbor. That server at the restaurant. That second cousin we barely know. That child we tuck into bed every night. That college student we have over on Christmas. That teenaged friend. That single mother. That professor who says he doesn't believe in God. That mechanic at our work. That boss we cannot stand. That woman who has gossiped about us. That church member we avoid in the halls because they are so annoying. We all need His power. We all need His saving love. For such a time as this, we determine and declare: *I am His, and I will speak up.*

> *Serving God with His holy courage burning inside changes us into less fearful people.*

## The Wisdom to Speak

I can't tell you how many times I wished I had thought through something better before putting it in writing or letting it come out of my mouth. Like the time I commented, "Congratulations, baby mama" to the poor woman who had probably just had some MSG in her Chinese food the night before and was a little bloated but definitely not pregnant. We've all experienced this at one point: our good sense being outrun by our tongue.

I know it may seem strange for me to have just spent the last few pages imploring us to speak up and now advising caution to us in this speaking, but both are necessary. We must speak up for Jesus. We must go on record for our faith. And we must also be wise in this so we speak in such a way that the ultimate goal is salvation, not self-gratification. There must be a spiritual point to our speaking.

The truth is, most of us have a hard time at some point with the difference, mainly because we are so used to speaking our minds as the world tells us to, quickly, self-confidently, and without regard, instead of prayerfully and with great consideration as God exhorts (both Proverbs and James say a lot about this). The two are not the same. The trouble with speaking our minds like this is that our minds are rickety and unreliable—sometimes cloudy and noisy with popular thought, selfish gain, and negative drumbeats not taken captive and given over to God to clean up. The last thing the cause of Christ needs is for more of us to speak without regard. We have had plenty of that. We need God's wisdom in being His mouthpiece. There is responsibility in our role as His representative.

Think about it on a very pedestrian life level. What company in the world would tolerate a reckless representative of its brand? We want the dress, the speech, the everything to be consistent to the brand...so people know what to expect...so everyone is communicating the same thing from the heart and vision of the CEO or founder. God has standards for the way we conduct ourselves as His representatives. To bypass this and speak from a personal place is pride and mistrust of Him. It is not our right, nor is it effective for the Kingdom.

Here is the litmus test: When entering an important discussion or debate, is there a spiritual point? Will your words draw or point people to Jesus? If yes, speak up. If not, keep silent. The other stuff we can hash out in private venues or on our bedroom floor, with God. (If you only knew how many things God and I have hashed out.) This is about godly guardrails for us as believers, and at times we all need reminders as we travel together in this loud, humanistically biased world.

I've written my own list of sorts, to counsel myself in times I need the wisdom to speak—and because I want the best for you too, I share them with you now as points to remember:

1. Freedom of speech is huge, and culture is something we cannot avoid. So I'm not a proponent of sand-head-burying.

2. People come into every single situation with a level of bias, be it a childhood issue, a relationship experience, a hurt by the Church, etc. We cannot help this. It is life. So, while I respect the right to have and express human opinion, I do not let it govern my life because it's not completely trustworthy. Jesus is the only One always consistent and pure.

3. Just because we can speak up does not mean we should. I'm not sure any of us are ever changed by yet another opinion just for opinion's sake.

4. Jumping on bandwagons or strategizing about how to become more popular through our words is manipulation, not conviction. Steer far, far away from this.

5. I've wanted on many occasions to react to something, but I've never regretted remaining silent and doing work to combat my burden or conviction behind the scenes to see change.

6. The best thing I've ever done behind the scenes to help something change is pray. Nothing else works better. As I wrote in my book *I Want God*, "We talk too much and pray too little."

7. Yes, love is best. Is that still debatable? People aren't drawn to Christ, ever, by vitriol. But holiness and moral absolutes don't change with culture. And standing in that and speaking up for that with the Spirit leading the voice (the key) doesn't water down love. The end.

8. I don't ever want to be a "noisy gong" or "clanging cymbal" (1 Corinthians 13:1). My goal, though often I fall short: if there's no arrow to God with my words, I'm out.

9. We have to ask ourselves constantly before we speak up about an issue, "Is this the best use of my time right now?" Sometimes, because of the burden God has placed on our hearts, it will be a yes. But more times than not, it's a no. Weighing in on an issue I could better use my time praying about it is a clear choice to pray more than speak.

I know I'm not the only one who struggles sometimes to have the wisdom to know when to speak and what to go on record about. I find Jesus in this gift of community with the Church, and I share these thoughts now to speak back to me, to convict my own heart, to be used by God to help guide us as we seek in a flesh body to influence culture and lead people to Him. This is a big task to ask of human people, how well I know. And how quickly it can get muddled. It's easy to want to react and think our words vital to every conversation. But the bottom line must become that we do not speak just for speaking sake. Maturity and Spirit control, which go against our natural grain, are marks of the warrior boots believer, the Jesus strong life.

As a follower of Jesus Christ, though we all operate in America with free speech, speaking is not a rights issue in the Kingdom of God but a responsibility issue. Will it lead people to Christ? Ultimately, will it help guide people to a saving relationship with Him by our representation? Will we influence as salt and light by becoming a person others regard as wise and listen to in times of need? We are all influenced by someone. With our words, as His mouthpiece, can that be me or you? We need some good people. God's looking for some good people to step up. We who take Jesus seriously should shudder in thought about ever saying anything that He would not ordain or approve, just as we should shudder in thought over staying silent about Him. That is gospel accountability. That is loving and honoring our Savior. He never speaks out of turn or lets His words get the best of Him. That's us. But in that, let us not fear speaking, but speak boldly and loudly for the Kingdom things that matter. When we ground our words in Him, we cannot go wrong.

So let's reserve our going on record for the things that will draw people to Christ and lead them to the saving relationship He offers. That way we aren't speaking so much people tune us out. Before we speak, let's give ourselves the Best Choice Test back in chapter 3—"Is this wise? Is this about me? Is this God's best?"—and pray, pray, *pray*.

And just in case this is now or has ever been a point of question: telling people about what Jesus did on the cross is not something we need to pray about. It is a command, a right now, go on record, to do. But what we think about cultural debates? Pontificating all our theologies and interpretations of what Jesus is thinking and doing in other people's lives? That is a different story. Let us tread prayerfully in that.

As always, the final and wisest words come from God Himself—the words to tell us what kind of representative He's looking for, what He doesn't jive with, and what earthly rewards this rep's godly efforts will ultimately produce:

> Take a good look at my servant. I'm backing him to the hilt. He's the one I chose, and I couldn't be more pleased with him. I've bathed him with my Spirit, my life. He'll set everything right among the nations. He won't call attention to what he does with loud speeches or gaudy parades. He won't brush aside the bruised and the hurt and he won't disregard the small and insignificant, but he'll steadily and firmly set things right. He won't tire out and quit. He won't be stopped until he's finished

his work—to set things right on earth. Far-flung ocean islands wait expectantly for his teaching (Isaiah 42:1-4 MSG).

Oh, Jesus, *I hear You.* May You say this, too, about us.

---

*Yes to courage. Yes to rising. Yes to strength.*

---

## Marching On

Sometimes you will be loved in your speaking out and sometimes you will be hated. And in either space, it can never be about you. This is one of the most valuable things we can remember as we move forward with our warrior boots, Jesus strong, going-on-record life.

Our voice won't please everyone. Honestly, it won't please even almost everyone, and it really shouldn't or likely we are speaking a placating, vacuous message. We have to keep narrowing in on our focus to just please God. This is not an excuse to be reckless in speech, for goodness' sake, since no one can tell us straight from God's mouth what pleases Him so it's easy to brush off accountability or even criticism with this crutch of *you aren't God and you can't judge me.* Yes, this is true, but we have to be more mature than using that to slide out from under things. Our focus to just please God is meant to hold us to a higher standard, not a lower one.

Mainly, friends, our speaking life, our living life is to be about just marching on—staying in the pocket with God despite all else and moving forward. We must march on, in the power of God. We must march on, even in the midst of a painful journey. March on in preaching the gospel. March on with telling ourselves and others the truth from an immaculate heart of love. We need to march on in the warrior boots that being a child of God provides for us in unstable times. In trying times. In times that are really uphill and more difficult than we expected. We stay in the journey, like my friend Monty says, which may sound cliché and small, but to stay in the journey in a way that we are present and growing and engaged instead of coasting and settling and checking out is a huge thing. It's the call of God on our lives to press on and move forward. Really, do we have a choice?

This is why we must answer the call of God for readiness. This is why we have no choice but to put our warrior boots on and learn how to walk Jesus strong, even if we've never truly walked this way before. I believe it is possible. I know, because there have been times in my life when I didn't want to keep marching and by the grace and power of God, I did. You who have had babies go to heaven and you who have endured the unspeakable evil of abuse and sexual exploitation…you who have experienced racism and mental abuse and retaliation and unfairness and brutality…you who were told you were nothing and have never felt loved…you who stuck a needle in your arm looking for relief…you who eat out of control and your weight kills your spirit inside and you who purge food or hoard things or don't want to wake up in the morning sometimes, the burdens are so heavy…you know, if you are still here, about the power of marching on.

All of us at times have not wanted to keep marching on to the drumbeat of life. It's too hard and too scary. People act crazy and unstable, and we don't feel safe. All of it, I know. This is why our old strategy to just take life as it comes, respond to what life throws at us, truly will not work. We have to make some decisions in our life to survive better than that, right now.

And as we read the song of Deborah in Judges 5, may we hear the melody of the battle cry…for strength, for help from God, almighty power, truth, and hope, *oh glorious and righteous hope* in these words:

> March on with courage, my soul!…May those who love
> you rise like the sun in all its power (verses 21,31).

Isn't this just the point? That we not only march through this life but march through this life with courage. That we rise, even from the lowest possible place, full and bright and strong. Yes to courage. Yes to rising. Yes to strength. In these difficult times, we desperately need these things right now. So we must ask the only One who can help us.

*God, hear these, our cries, right now. We cry out for courage. We cry out for Your arms to help us rise. We cry out for strength, in a way we have never been strong before. We go on record declaring to the evil one that we will not be taken down or taken under by his schemes. We declare that we will not stay silent to the Kingdom things that matter. We declare that we will not believe the lies of the enemy that we are destined to the slavery of fear. We declare that we are marching on, doing it Your way. We say yes, to putting our warrior boots on and walking Jesus strong, once and for all. You've told us in Your Word this is possible, if we will trust and honor You. Now, today, we are holding You to it.*

Amen and amen.

WEEK 5

# I WILL GO ON RECORD

**Take a Deeper Dive: Acts 6–7**

**10 minutes:** Welcome. Share about a time you had to put your money where your mouth was (funny or serious).

**10 Minutes:** Intro to chapter through Video Teaching with Lisa (outline and videos available online at www.warriorbootsbook.com)

**35 Minutes:** Small Group Discussion (Take the first 10 minutes to answer privately, then the last 25 to discuss as a group.)

1. Talk about the life of Stephen. What prepared him to go on record for his faith, even in the face of death?

2. How important are a fierce love and fierce loyalty in walking strong in this world?

3. What does going on record for your faith look like? What is an everyday example of this?

4. How big of a role does having the wisdom to speak have in going on record? Why is this so crucial?

5. Do most believers have the "marching on" mentality in life or is our tendency to retreat and cower in the face of obstacles and bad news? What will change that?

**Prayer:** God, we learn from the example of Stephen and the martyrs who have gone before—help us have the courage like them to go on record for You. Where our love is not fierce, make it fiercer. Where our loyalty is not fierce, strengthen our bond. We take responsibility for sometimes speaking out of turn and turning people off to the gospel. Forgive us. Help us march on from here, putting our money where our mouth is with wisdom in faith. Yes and amen.

**Bonus Home Helps:**

1. Do a word study of *speak* from Scripture.

2. Memorize and meditate on Romans 10:10, "With the mouth confession is made unto salvation" (NKJV).

3. Memorize and meditate on Judges 5:21 and 31: "March on with courage, my soul!...May those who love you rise like the sun in all its power."

4. Make your own "wisdom to speak" exhortation list, listing at least three things. Ask a friend to make a list and then get together over coffee to share and discuss. (Iron sharpens iron, my friend!)

5. Ask someone close to you to pray for you to have the courage and wisdom to share the gospel and live out this five-word (*I Will Go on Record*) declaration in your life.

# Journal

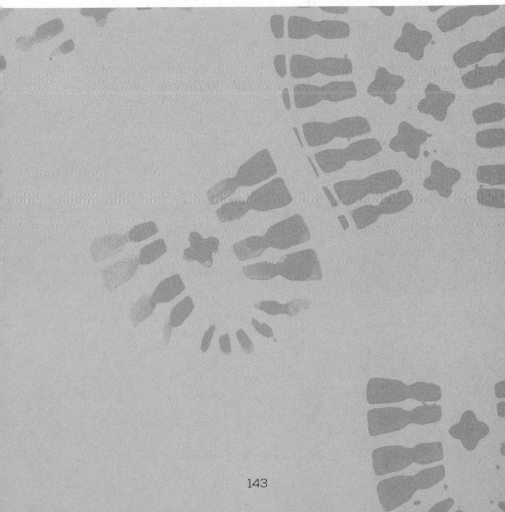

# PART THREE

# BOOTS OF TRUST

# I WILL CHOOSE GOD

You can make this choice by loving the LORD
your God, obeying him, and committing yourself
firmly to him. This is the key to your life.
**DEUTERONOMY 30:20**

There is none all good as thou art: with thee I can
live without other things, for thou art God all-
sufficient, and the glory, peace, rest, joy of the
world is a creaturely, perishing thing in comparison
with thee. Help me to know that he who hopes for
nothing but thee, and for all things only for thee,
hopes truly, and that I must place all my happiness
in holiness, if I hope to be filled with all grace.
**VALLEY OF VISION, "FULLNESS"**

I dreamed of being a gymnast when I was a little girl jumping on
trampolines in small-town Oklahoma. Until one day I watched
an Olympic gymnast being interviewed on TV, talking about how
much she had to sacrifice to reach her goal of the gold medal, and
I realized it was all too much work for me. She had dreams, plans,
goals, and a single focus: that moment when she would stand on
the riser and her hard work would be rewarded with a shiny medal
placed around her neck.

But first, she would have to be willing to live a separate, solo life
without everyone always understanding or sharing her enthusiasm
for the goal she was working toward. She would have to say no to
dinners and hangouts and hours of lying beside a pool in order to

train. She would have to forgo Disney vacations where everyone in the group wears the same florescent T-shirt and say yes to the hot, smelly gym instead. She would have to say no to the prom or movie dates on the weekend if it was the same weekend as a gymnastics meet. In order to achieve a goal so great, she had to be willing to give up the other things—sometimes the important things too—because that was the way of the solo-living, greatness-seeking life. She made her choice, and nothing could get in the way of it, and nothing ever did.

*It is the same for the way of the greatness-seeking Jesus life.*

What about you, my friend? Do you long to live a life of greatness, as I suspect you do? We may not want to be great like an Olympian, but all of us long to live a great life—one that matters, one that influences people, one that accomplishes something. A life of greatness is a life that honors God. As followers of Jesus Christ, we, the believers in Him, made an agreement with our lives at the moment of salvation to live singularly and solely for Him.

I sense we forget about this agreement sometimes and hold the commitment loosely. It was our choice then and now—to seal our future and determine the mission statement of our life. This means our training for heaven has officially begun. And in the interim of reaching it, we will have to keep that heavenly goal as the only focus. Other things will have to fade. We don't have to worry about what to do with our days now—this was decided for us when we chose to accept the free gift of salvation. We said yes to our goal of eternity and no to everything else. Like the Olympian with the commitment to the solo life, so the commitment to live with a solo focus on God was and is our choice. Everything in life is about choosing. Everything in our spiritual life will come down to whether we choose God or not. It is a singular choosing.

Everything in life is about choosing. Everything in our spiritual life will come down to do we choose God, or not. It is a singular choosing.

*All of us long to live a great life—one that matters, one that influences people, one that accomplishes something.*

I should point out, though, that community matters and family matters, and we are not on this walk alone. So, in that way, the thought of living a solo life seems to be a bit incongruous even with Scripture (Genesis 2:18; 1 Corinthians 12; Proverbs 27:17). It's true that the Church is the greatest example of how life is meant to be lived linking arms, finding encouragement, and yes, feeling humanly loved. I've been hurt by the Church before, like many others, but I could never quite quit it because despite the hurt, I knew I couldn't survive this journey alone. I didn't have to like the way the Church acted sometimes to believe in its importance. (This is indeed a good thing.) At the very least, I knew my life would be less rich without the understanding and companionship (and occasionally the church fellowships with covered dishes) of people who had chosen the same commitment in life that I had. The older I get, the more I know for sure that I never want to do life without the Church. Otherwise, to believe in a God I can't see and keep the faith I need to have in Him with the sway and seduction of the world pulling it's hardest against that would be far more difficult. There's just something about a bond with people of like faith unlike any other to help us through.

To do life without people of likeminded faith and community, our very own spiritual brothers and sisters, is to take out from under us the very support we need to walk through life. No one is strong all the time. God gave us each other to help us through—the call or text that comes just in time, the reminder of a verse we've forgotten, the lifestyle we've committed to and share, the prayer prayed on our behalf, the understanding in the eyes and hugs and smiles that those who do not follow Jesus can't give us in the same way. What a gift to have each other, and what a travesty to deny ourselves the gift, ignoring its value.

Even deeper, the struggle for us in this idea of solo living is that God ordained families, and it is honoring to Him to care for them, nurture them, invest in them, pay them close attention. We've seen what happens when people neglect family, and it never turns out well. Divorce for couples who don't tend the gardens of relationship along the way and eventually the garden is nothing but unruly weeds, unable to be handled. Jobs taking over and kids taking a backseat to them at the time they need emotional and physical things the most. Elderly parents being ushered into our invisibility and deemed irrelevant to our daily lives, sitting alone in a rocking chair with nary a loved one coming to visit. How these things break God's heart. No, we must, indeed, care for our families in the way He intends. Surely God wouldn't call us to live the solo life with Him to the neglect of our families.

*True.* He has given us the responsibility to see that they are loved well, served well, honored well, valued well, fiercely protected, and taken care of. But we have to reconcile this inner struggle that to be most about God, even above our families, is not impossible or wrong—it is, in fact, right. It will take godly wisdom, prayer, and discernment in every situation that seems to be at odds to maneuver this. But the interesting thing is that most things in life will not be that confusing. If we walk with God, He gives us a sense of what we are supposed to do. This is where the idea that God knows the heart comes into play in a gratitude-inducing way. Because there is a heart intention that God sees and values above all that tends to compensate at times for our human lack to always properly carry life out. It's not charity work to have our heart be right with God; it's sanity saving. It's how we ensure things stay in sync with Him, even when our flesh fails us.

I can relate to the perspective of author Francis Chan on this subject, a husband and father with a full ministry life as well:

One of my biggest struggles is making sure I don't love my kids too much! If I'm not careful, they can become the chief recipients of my love and affections rather than Christ…Our kids must be taught and shown that the world does not revolve around them—it revolves around Jesus. We live for Him.[1]

The greatest life is one of singular choice and commitment to the Kingdom of God. It's saying no to even the good things to say yes to God. It's the *everyone else is a far-off second* mentality. It's the eye on the goal, narrowed and intent, to where everything in the daily simply exists to line up to the greater life purpose. In this way, again, we take out so much flux and complication. We move away from reactionary living because commitments are immune to the latest news or horrific happening. We do ourselves an enormous favor by making strong commitments. Those commitments simplify our schedules and let people know what to expect from us, even our very own kids.

> *It's not charity work to have our heart be right with God; it's sanity saving.*

Without commitment, we will never walk through this hard life any way but scared and full of doubt, because emotions will rule us instead of absolutes. This is why the *no boundaries, no rules* way of life ruins us. Freedom without moral and spiritual absolutes turns us into nervous wrecks.

The hard irony is that in many ways we've let ourselves go, Christians, while we have mistakenly thought we were cultivating a better self. We've let ourselves accept things that are beneath our spiritual heritage. It's not that we are better than this—we are dust, nothing— but God is infinitely better than this, and to live at odds with who He is doesn't make sense. We've allowed grasping and freaking out to be an acceptable way of living. It's no wonder you can't tell us apart from the nonbelievers. All of us walk the same kind of unsteady. *Below our potential.*

Jesus has a remedy for this. It's called choosing the solo life, which gives us the character to face crises and the will not to quit. I'm not trying to diminish our hardships: they are regular and plenty. But choosing God is the best choice we will ever make for the best life we will ever have. Because it is a sure choice. There has never been anything more sure. There will never be anything more sure. There will never be a better deal or a better option we should have waited a week on before we chose. We never have to feel stupid for choosing God. We never have to feel duped. We never have to feel like we invested in something that is empty or won't end well. We can sleep at night with confidence and peace, and this is exactly what He says will be the case in our choosing of Him: "If you lie down, you will not be afraid; when you lie down, your sleep will be sweet" (Proverbs 3:24 ESV). When we choose God, we make a choice to walk through life confidently with the knowledge we've made the right choice. Because He and He alone never changes, the choice for God for strength, guidance, and protection is the right choice, forever.

> The Lord can be trusted to make you strong and protect you from harm (2 Thessalonians 3:3 CEV).

## The 1-2-3 of Choosing

In what I believe to be one of the best recorded human speeches of all time, given by Moses in the powerful book of Deuteronomy, he gives the clearest outline of what our choice for God will look like in three short words: *love, obey,* and *commit.*

> You can make this choice by loving the LORD your God, obeying him, and committing yourself firmly to him. This is the key to your life (30:20).

This speech was inspired by God Himself, so we have to believe these are the things we need to know on the subject. I love how God recognizes our need for bottom-line, simple truth with the finite minds we have and the busy schedules we keep. Even this wording in this passage, so to the point, so clear, reminds me of how much He sees my life and longs to make Himself known to me in a way I can easily understand. Our Father, ever the Nurturer.

### Choose to Love

We've got to choose to love God. This sounds so simple, but it has proven in my life at times to be hard. I love God with exceptions and with my preferred spin. I love Him *if* He will tell me everything I want to know and *if* He'll do things when I want them and *if* He'll never allow me to go through anything hard. But that can't be love because in that is so much of me. Pure love for God will never respond with an *if* or a *when*.

The kind of love I need is the kind that doesn't change with my circumstance and doesn't get forgotten or watered down when it works better for me. But I'm not there yet. I know that in this world and in my days to come that my intensity of love for God must go to a new level. The choice to love God may be a no-brainer, but it is not to be taken lightly or thought of as simple. It's not natural for us to love anyone but ourselves, and yes, that includes God. We know He died for us and rescued us and we should love Him for that and on one level we do, but that is easily forgotten in our everyday life. When there is something we want more, we quietly set Him aside so we can have it. Even the Israelites, God's own chosen people, who were miraculously rescued from the Egyptians, and who were miraculously rescued over and over again for the next 40 years, still had to be reminded to love Him. Even with the One who has done everything for us, over and over again, love doesn't come naturally. That is why He calls it a choice.

So, how do we choose to love God in a daily, practical sense?

- We push aside fear and excuse and go serve Him in some way that goes against our natural desire or comfort level.

Saying no to our flesh shows a love for God beyond
ourselves.

- We volunteer with a group of people we have the hardest
time loving. Remember, when we love other people we
show God we love Him—especially those He knows we
are not naturally drawn to love. (If we were, it wouldn't
be sacrifice.)

- We pick up and study our Bible. It's true—God values
quality time. We can see this as a chore or we can see
this as a way to show Jesus we love Him, as our prayer
life will also do. We've heard this all before, but that
doesn't make it small or nullified. If it falls on deaf ears
and we skim over it, shame on us. It's not an old concept; it's just the most tried and true concept that has
ever worked for every situation. (Lest we forget—studying the Bible is not predominately to please God. It's the
discipline that will help our life become strong. Everything we need to know is found in the Word of God.)

- We respond to God quickly when He impresses things
on our heart, instead of dragging our feet, justifying, or
white-knuckling it past the moment. The truth is, God
knows we love Him by our willingness to obey. He
wants and deserves immediate obedience.

- We pray. How can we stay away from a conversation
with the One who matters, who helps, who makes sense
in the midst of our mixed-up life? The more we choose
to have one on ones with God, the more we show Him
our love.

- We share His heart for the Church. First John 5:1
reminds us, "Everyone who believes that Jesus is the
Christ has become a child of God. And everyone who
loves the Father loves his children, too."

- We go on record. A vocal faith shows God we love Him. He requires us to profess our love for Him before man (Matthew 10:32).

- We tithe. People get sideways and crazy when we start to talk about things like giving our 10 percent tithe to the church. But it is an act of service to God, above all. It's not really about the money—it's all about the heart, which either withholds or gives generously. God set it up this way and had His reasons. Our financial sacrifice is really our gain because it strengthens our relationship with Jesus.

- We take care of widows and orphans. Taking care of someone involves aspects like heart (always), time, financials, and yes, physically housing them too. It's our job to pray through *how* God wants to use us to fulfill this command, not pray *if* He wants to use us, which He has already made clear in the book of James. We must remain open to the fact that God may ask us to be inconvenienced in order for this command to love to be lived out. If we find ourselves justifying our disobedience, we need to ask ourselves at the core why we do not love Him enough to obey—perhaps it is because we do not really trust Him or we have a root of self. (This is where I dare say every rejection of the gospel on our part lies.) If we have never ministered to these two groups, how deep can our love for God be since He called these groups specifically out by name? (I rest this case under personal conviction.)

- Most of all, our choice to love God will be a choice to preach the gospel. How many of us have gone days, months, years, ever, without leading one person to the saving knowledge of Him? And we say we love Him? At its depth, if we peel back all the layers, this is not about our fear or our insecurity or our respecting other people or proper timing—it's about our lack of love for God that in reverse would drive us crazy in our bodies until we let it out by sharing the news about Whom we love. This is hard truth, I know. But our choice to love God has enormous stakes and is essential to putting our warrior boots on and walking strong. (And remember, in chapter 3, we already committed to tell ourselves the truth.)

*Obedience to God has to be
about choice, not mood.*

### Choose to Obey

We've got to choose to obey God. It is a choice, not a feeling. We don't always like the practical part of our relationship with God, and due to our sinful nature, we will likely often want to say no to His commands. Let's be real, if I waited to cook dinner until I felt like it, my family would starve. When my husband used to get service calls from large and important customers for repair parts (he's a small business owner of heavy equipment repair and service) in the middle of the night and have to get out of bed at 2:00 a.m. to drive until 4:00 a.m. and then go to regular work hours a couple of hours later, he never, ever wanted to. But he got up and went because his commitments to take care of our family and keep the business productive and afloat came before his feelings. And in some especially lean financial years, I'm so grateful he did.

There's way too much emphasis on our feelings in this world, which should tell us exactly why it's in such disarray. Humans are not capable of determining things based on our feelings. When we have, it's turned chaotic.

So obedience to God has to be about choice, not mood. If it's all about our feelings, we stay in an emotional rut. Fortunately, there is a way to make it easier on ourselves: we keep saying yes to God even when we don't feel it (eventually, though our flesh will always fight it to a degree, it does become somewhat easier after time), and we refuse to put ourselves in situations that would cause us to violate our commitment to His Word.

We don't go to the hotel—we won't be able to sleep with the other person.

We write out the check for our tithe amount as soon as we get our paycheck and don't factor that money in for the rest of our weekly/monthly spendings—we set ourselves up to obey the call to tithe.

We change the subject when we start to gossip about a friend—we save ourselves from sinning.

These are just a few examples and, at first, things that may seem simple. But simple can be life altering when it keeps us from getting tangled in a much more complicated web, and we have to take an honest look at how many of these helpful things we really do. How often do we set up guardrails? Or do we much more often let life go by and feel good about how we are doing the best we can when in reality we aren't doing much to support our choice to obey God?

Our lifestyle of obedience will be a direct result of how much we set ourselves up for it. The praying life will be more able to obey than the non-praying life. The person who sets up the guardrails in advance will be more able to obey than the one who drives with no healthy fear of the open shoulder. When we become of the age and ability to choose, we set up the life we end up having. This is true of people who floss their teeth religiously (result: less cavities) and people who do parkour like crazy people (result: probable broken bones) and people who make a choice to obey God and then travel only down the road that will keep us going in the right direction.

### Choose to Commit

We've already talked about commitment, so I'm hopeful by now you are convinced of how truly important it is. Yet when I talk to people across the United States, in retreats and conferences and over coffee, one of the recurring angsts of our Christian life is how hard it is to stay on fire for God.

I get it. In the midst of insanely packed schedules and needs pressing on every side, to stay in a spiritual place all the time is difficult. We are all human. None of us go around singing worship songs 24 hours a day, nor would any of us want others to. (I added that last part in case you're tempted to do this around me.) I am drawn to people who aren't perfect in the sense that we want Christians to be—people who speak openly of their bad day or how they cussed when they dropped a hammer on their toe or behaved poorly with the receptionist at the doctor's office when she was rude. (*Ahem.*) It's not about some Shekinah glow around our head or our over-the-top perfect life. At least, I'm counting on that to be true.

At a certain point we have to ask ourselves if we want to continue to settle for a hot and cold Jesus life and if we can really stomach one more year of the spiritual roller coaster. Many of us drag on year after year with an unfulfilled spiritual life. At some point, we have to choose to do something else. If we believe that all things are indeed possible with God, we have hope, then, that our spiritual life is not doomed to stagnation and inconsistency.

God mentions commitment in the Deuteronomy passage as a way to get it together spiritually. It is the tipping point decision between "life and death, between blessings and curses," according to Moses in verse 19. Those are incredibly important distinctions. When we are truly tired of being on the spiritual roller coaster, we will do something about it. Until then, we are only a little weary and a lot on the fence.

A true commitment to God is a thorough, overarching commitment over every area of our life, and the outflow of that is a vibrant spiritual connection. This is the kind of commitment that lasts, and commitment is what keeps us off the highs and lows of Christian living. God delights in our kept promises. He dances and has a party over them. Commitments to Him have never come cheap—we can read history about the Bible heroes and martyrs and know this is the truth—so He holds our commitment to Him in the highest of regard…honoring it, even within the understanding of the command.

Commitment is every single day, every single moment. We live commitment. We breathe it. We don't get a shot at salvation that is good for four to six years like a vaccine. We don't get it renewed like a passport. It's not enough to say, *Yes, I accepted You as Savior, Jesus,* and then go on our own way. It has to be about *Today, I choose You again.* And in this situation where I could gossip about a friend, *I choose You, God,* which means I won't gossip because God wouldn't like it. And in this situation where I could look at porn and no one would even know, *I won't because I choose You, God,* because it will hurt both of our hearts.

These are the daily choosings. They may look like a choice to gossip or watch porn or overeat or lie to a friend or steal something that isn't ours, but really, they are all a choice for or against God. When we see our life through this lens, decisions look different.

And if there is to be a sacrifice in all our choosing, let us not look at the denial but at the better that has come from it. For in our love and our obedience and our commitment, we become grounded, steady, solid as a rock. These things are again natural results. They are the things we really want, the things that help us live and survive and yes, thrive too. It's not our figuring out how to get more brave or lifting more spiritual weights by joining in every Bible study we can get our hands on. It's in the choosing of our God and choosing Him over and over again, personally, publicly, privately, when no one else but Him knows.

### Just the Facts

Right now, my husband and I are operating in a *just the facts, please* stage of our parenting. This came up recently when one of our teenagers claimed to be "doing great" in an area we knew he was struggling.

It had been happening more and more, these claims without tangible proof, and we had grown more tired of it than shoes thrown all over the floor. (Parents, I know you feel me.) We had solid proof that our child's assessment of the situation was incorrect. Either we were being lied to or our child was suffering from a vast lack of self-awareness.

This newly defined type of parenting came out of necessity, which as parents know is when most of our accidental parenting brilliance occurs: we are squeezed into trying something that winds up working when we are at our wits' end. And clearly, we were being squeezed. Clearly, we had to try a different approach.

"From now on," my husband said, "we will go just on the facts to determine how well you are doing. I don't want to know what you think about how well you are doing in school; I will know by your grades. I don't want to know how well you think you're doing in your sports; I will know by how much you play in the game."

At first, my maternal instincts fought against this. I want my kids to know we value what they think. But my husband was right. My son's feelings had been skewing the reality of what was going on in his life. He believed his emotions were the ultimate truth.

The epidemic of parental concern over our children's every feeling is staggering, and as a result, we are seeing a generation raised up to cave to their every mood and whim. We wonder why they don't take out the trash or do their homework or clean up that mess of a room. *They don't feel like it.* And then we wonder later on why they choose not to go to church or stick it out in a tough job situation or a tough marriage moment. It's directly tied to the message they have been allowed to receive that feelings are the main thing, not honoring commitments. In the effort to have constantly happy children, we have created the thing we fear—that our kids will be entitled, that they will not know how to say no to themselves and not listen to an authority that doesn't let them negotiate. (Which we know, in the end, leaves them not happy people at all.) Responsible parenting balances human respect with natural hierarchy. The Father Himself models this in His relationship with us.

Parent or not, I trust you hear the bigger point. We *all* do this— hold our feelings in too high of a regard and base important decisions on them as a result. In this skewed reality, vital things become diminished and ignored. Insignificant things become overblown. Someone doesn't return our text for a few days and we rack our brain trying to figure out why they obviously don't care about us or what we have done to turn them off. We create full scenarios in our heads within mere minutes, which are based in little to no reality. Relationships have been lost over this, ridiculous as it seems. We know feelings aren't the way to run our life, but still we often let them run us around.

If we are going to walk strong in this world, I can't emphasize strongly enough the importance of choice. Choice over perception. Choice over cultural trend. We don't become robots or live in mental metal cages. We anchor our lives to something sure and right. The call to put our warrior boots on is the call to make wise, prayerful choices based on the Word of God rather than operating life on knee-jerk assessments in crisis moments. We shouldn't settle for that. It's a less-than-best way to live.

When it comes to our present and future, our ability to hope, our fears right now, we've got to start basing our reality on spiritual facts. It sounds rigid to some degree, I know, and I thought that at first too, about the "facts-only" parenting. (Which, by the way, is not the way we've always parented, but it is what this particular season with three teens and their complexities requires.) Surprisingly, it's eliminated a lot of stress. Most of us would love nothing more than to figure out a way to make our lives less stressful. We can: we start to live a life of *just the facts.* The facts always fall in Jesus' favor. As His child, the facts always benefit us.

## Outfitting Our Life (to Support Our Choice)

Passion without preparation is a good intention designed to fade.

I've seen people so passionate at one time about God I never, ever thought they would be the one to leave the faith and walk away. And yet give them enough time in the pressure cooker of life, have them live in an environment that doesn't foster that, see them get entangled in sin and never turn to repentance and change, and that passion eventually turns cold. Before we get too comfortable in our judgment recliner, may I remind you that this description could be of any one of us. All of us have the human capability to become spiritually lifeless. All of us can turn from passionate Jesus follower to Jesus follower who gave up or walked away. May we quake at this thought, that we, too, are but one flesh moment away of walking a godless path.

The reality is that unless we outfit our life to support our choices, our best choices will not sustain a secular high wind. There is a reason a nutritionist asks us to clean out the pantry and clear out all the junk before we start a healthy eating plan: because the choice to eat better will not easily be sustained without the environment supporting it. There's a reason scuba divers can't dive without the proper equipment and training. Only a fool would attempt a dive without careful prep work for it first. This is true of so many life things.

> *Passion without preparation is*
> *a good intention designed to fade.*

Choosing God is a logical, strategic life plan fueled by a heart of belief and passion. One without the other will cause the life to be out of balance. This is why good attendance in church has never helped a person be strong enough to go out in the world and lead someone to Christ. It's not enough, without the belief and passion driving it. And yet passion without proper order can't last. Our hands will raise in the air on Sunday to precious Jesus praise songs and then on Monday they will tuck into our pockets so we don't have to use them to serve. Love and passion and choice go together, my friends. Choosing the God life is the ultimate passionate life plan.

We *choose* to search for God, pursue and get to know Him, even though we already have Him in our heart. First Chronicles 16:11 tells us, "Search for the LORD and for his strength; continually seek him." We *choose* to believe God, even when the circumstantial proof is not there. We *choose* to hope, though things look dark. Don't ever let anyone tell you that these things aren't a choice. *They are.*

These mental determinations do not require support feelings, thank God. Many of us have made major life decisions claiming to be led by the heart, when in actuality, it's been feelings that have spoken up on the heart's behalf, leading us wrongly.

This reminds me of an episode on the once wildly popular TV series *The West Wing*, in which one of the characters has made a baseless accusation. Several other women are discussing it. "She said she knew it in her heart," says one of the women about the claim. "You know how many things I've been wrong about in my heart?" the other replies.[2] How well *I* know. How well I relate. I've decided many things in my life based on perceptions and assessments, and 99 percent of them have never worked out. My feelings have taken over for my heart and pushed good choices out. But I have never made a mental determination for God that failed me yet. This is the uniqueness of a Spirit-led life. Scripture does not have flux to it. No words of Jesus have ever been proven wrong.

In my own spiritual journey, I have had more highs and lows than I can count. There were times in my childhood that God was so close I would have sworn He was physically holding my hand. There were days in my young adulthood where I consumed Scripture more than food and passionately led strangers to Christ. But there have been painfully equal amounts of days that I forgot God completely. Some days even farther down the spiritual slide, I remembered Him and still chose sin and neglect. I won't ever be off the flesh journey of the spiritual life until I get to heaven. I've been a believer in Jesus for 38 blessed years, and I've only lived a handful of them with the understanding it is not about my spiritual perfection. I can't perfect my way into walking Jesus strong; I must live my life choosing it, over and over again. It is the same for you.

The best way I've found in those 38 years to support my passion for God—help it not fizzle out depending on circumstances—was to prepare my life, properly. Winging it simply will not work. (Tried that, no thanks.) I'm far too lazy and too self-centered, so I have to box myself in and then wrap the box with duct tape so there's no chance of escape.

We outfit our life to support our choice for God in three key ways. (Are you ready for this epic prep list? You have probably never heard it before. Insert sarcasm.)

**Read your Bible.** Read it when you're sad, read it when you're mad, read it when you don't want to know what it has to say, read it when you don't feel you understand it, read it when you would rather watch TV and you wonder what's the point. Read it, every day and often. You say to me, "But, Lisa, I already read my Bible." I say to you, "Good. Me too. Let's read it some more."

**Pray.** Don't talk about how important it is: do it. Do it right now. Stop reading this minute and pray. Pray when it's the last thing you want to do. Pray when you're sick of praying. Stop telling people you are praying for them as mere words and, instead, really pray for them. You say to me, "But, Lisa, I already pray." I say to you, "Good. Me too. Let's pray some more."

**Constantly put yourself in positions to see God's transformative work.** We know about prayer and we know about Bible reading, but this is the one key prep list item we may be sleeping on. Yet this sometimes hard, sometimes not as hard step has radically changed my spiritual life in a powerful way. The more we put ourselves in positions to see God move, the less willing we are to stay a stagnant, halfway Christian. The problem is, Satan is good at mental terrorism so he wins a lot in that space with us. He constantly whispers to us that something for God is too scary, too hard, requires a better person, and it's his way of sitting us down and shutting us up from the very start. It's especially his tactic with believers who have not been used to taking any kind of radical or faith-requiring step. He does this because he knows that were we ever to take that very first, hardest step and experience a moment where God showed up big, changed a person's life in front of us, took over our bodies and helped us do something with our mouth or feet or hands we are not normally able to do, we would want more of that. Then we wouldn't be able to unknow what we know. Then we wouldn't settle for the backseat in life but would be unsatisfied with anything but front-row, Kingdom-radical living. And he never, ever wants us to know.

It's a strategy of Satan's to stifle the expansion of the Kingdom, so we have to out-strategize him by putting ourselves in a position that probably at first will scare us to death in order to help defy it. Note: This being scared is completely normal for a big Jesus move or even a smaller one (really, big and small are our terms of measurement, not His). Expect it, then pray quickly when it shows up. You are in good company. Lots of us have done things for God scared. Putting our warrior boots on makes us able to do it anyway.

> *The more we put ourselves in positions to see God move, the less willing we are to stay a stagnant, halfway Christian.*

I've seen it happen in my friends who started doing foster care who used to be satisfied with sitting on couches and then chose to put themselves in a position to see God do something, really do something for once. Some days were a disaster. Some days were sweet. But in the end, none of the ups and downs mattered because they got to see God do God-sized things in their lives. They didn't become sold on foster care for foster care's sake; they became sold on a life dedicated to Him and how He shows up and does transformative work in and through normal, doing it scared and anyway people.

I've seen it happen in other friends who became missionaries who never wanted that kind of life and now crave it. I've seen it happen in really normal people who never did much before and now can't stop serving God in a downtown homeless ministry and don't want to. I've seen it happen over and over again, to people who simply choose to take their burning ember of passion, small flame as it might be, and stoke it by putting themselves in a position for God to blow up their whole flickering life in the best of ways. They forced themselves into still submission for the first time and let God show them something. And now they know. Now they have a different eye sparkle and outlook on life. Now their passion is supported. Passion that is supported by lifestyle does not easily wane.

And yes, too, I've seen it happen in me. Since I got up for the first time, scared to death to say yes to God to use me in His giftings, I can't unknow what has happened since. I can't unknow that He comes through for me in situations where I am inadequate. I can't unknow the times I've wrestled in prayer in a hotel room, about to speak and feeling like I will monumentally flop. I can't unknow that watching God unite hearts through readers like you and my pedestrian writer's pen of personal longing helps us both understand divine connection and thus, journey on, stronger. I can't unknow that He is the only thing to ever make me feel better when I'm in pain. I can't unknow that life without serving Him feels like a nothing life and makes me want to jump out of my skin.

This not being able to unknow has carried me far and wide and put me in situations my natural introvert fights like mad against. It's sent me to rehab facilities to talk to prostitutes and addicts, taken me to college campuses and homeless shelters and other parts of the world to preach the gospel that has so radically changed my life. Without what I can't unknow, I know I would settle for the shopping, hanging out, and just having fun life that I admit some-times my flesh still wants. Only what we can't unknow about God gives us the kind of strength to do any amazing thing.

I'll never forget coming back from Honduras after speaking to a group of women there—about 200, most of whom could not speak English and many of whom had walked hours with babies on a hip on a dusty gravel road to gather with our missionary group. A friend who found out about the trip said to me very sincerely, "Wow, Lisa, I didn't know you had a heart for Honduras. That's great."

My response to her, unplanned and straight from the heart: "It's not about Honduras for me. It's about seeing God do something somewhere I've never been and seen it before. I don't care where that is, to be honest. After going to Honduras, I do have a heart for those people. But it's not about Honduras, in particular, for me. It's about putting myself in a position to see God do something big." And this, my friends, has proven over and over to be true.

You want to grow your faith? Step into something that challenges you. You want to become Jesus strong? Do something you cannot do without God. This, friends, is a life strategy to get yourself off the spiritual roller coaster. When we are sick of this ever-fluid, reaction-ary, and unsure life, we will finally make this choice. When we are tired of the fizzling out of our passion, we will set up our life to ensure spiritual success. We will be only as spiritually accomplished as our preparation before we set out on the journey. We've got to have the proper supplies. We've got to create a conducive environment.

The best of intentions for our spiritual life will not give us the strength and readiness we need. Our life has to back up our spo-ken desires for God. Then we will combine our passion with a really good plan, and man, what a powerful combination that is.

*You want to grow your faith? Step into something that challenges you. You want to become Jesus strong? Do something you cannot do without God.*

## Choosing Sanity and Stability

The choice for God has saved many a man's and woman's life from wandering aimlessly without purpose. That choice has removed clouds of darkness in minds and hearts. It has lifted chains from lives. Choosing God keeps us sane and stable, two things we are constantly in search of that nothing else is able to provide. We are tired of losing our minds over all the things that worry us, griefs and injustices we cannot make right. We are tired of living life out of balance and unsteady on our feet. When we become sick enough of these things, we become the best candidates for choosing God.

God doesn't get mad about being the last thing we've tried, the final hope, the end of our rope—He just wants us to at some point come. His desire for us is that it not be this way—this *let me try other things first* life—because He knows that in that process of not choosing well we will incur unnecessary heartache that we could have avoided had we chosen Him sooner. Sin leads to suffering. As pastor James MacDonald said, "When God says, 'Don't,' He really means, 'Don't hurt yourselves.'"[3] I'm not sure in our daily lives we stop to give God enough credit for just how deeply He cares.

It's not that life is perfect when we have God—we know this from the remembrance of our brothers and sisters across the globe who suffer for the cause of Christ…the Christians we know even here in comfortable America who face places of fear and distress. While our flesh may beg us for the perfect life, what most of us really long for is the Jesus solid life, which is different and, even in the midst of hard, inexplicably *possible*. All the Jesus solid life things are the things that come from within, which would explain why the world apart from Him thrashes and despairs. Living well is our choice, in the sense that a life lived well is a life lived for God. Living free is our choice. Living stable and sane. The idea that we have the ability to choose our own level of sanity and stability in this world despite these crazy times is powerful. It doesn't mean we control the world; it means we won't be victims of an out-of-our-control world.

The world can continue in its tailspin, but we don't have to spin with it. This is some of the best news I have ever mined because many days I feel like the world's victim, and I don't want that role anymore.

*It's not that life is perfect when we have
God; it's that life is solid and in order.*

Our strength in this life will be determined by how soon we choose God. When we choose Him above all the other things, immediately a new power source is engaged and our life begins to alter. Choosing God is not a plan B. It is the only choice, whether we arrive at it early or late. It all depends on how much damage we want to do to ourselves before we open the hospital door to the only place we can truly get well, in our minds, in our lives. Don't underestimate the power of the sanity and stability of God.

I cannot live without the sanity and stability of God. I've tried, and I've collected the scars to prove it. Without the sanity of God, I am in a no-way-out labyrinth of mental angst—I cannot live with the knowledge of a world that has it so mixed up and all the ways that effects the people I love most. I cannot live with injustices I have read about, pictures I can't unsee, the knowledge of what-ifs and ways I can't make certain things make sense—without the sanity of God, I can't make it.

I cannot live without the stability of God, for without it, I am left to the mercy of other people's poor decisions, having the burden to stay standing on my own two feet after being abandoned and helplessly watching while things are being taken without my permission. I buckle in my flesh under these kinds of hardships. Without the stability of God, I go down.

As I talk to people in all walks of life, I've come to learn that one of our greatest wishes is to be okay no matter what happens. We just want to be okay, and we want someone to tell us we will be, no matter what. If we get a no on a life plan when we desperately want a yes, will we be okay? If we get rejected by a person we long to love, will we be okay? And God forbid, if we lose things or people we love by destruction or death, will we be okay even then? These questions are universal. We all think about them, at least some of the time. We can encourage each other about this, but in the end, we can't make each other this kind of promise.

> *Don't underestimate the power of*
> *the sanity and stability of God.*

Only the sanity and stability of God will help us be okay even if these difficult, life-crushing things come. On either end of the difficulty spectrum and in everything in between, life is only okay with God.

Are you tired of reactionary living—hearing the news and reverting to fear and frenzy? *Choose God.* This is what a person in warrior boots will do. The best combat of reactionary living is the grounded life. We choose whether or not we will have it. Isn't that amazing news? The world doesn't get to decide how well we are. It never has, for the followers of Jesus Christ.

I am reminded of this and the importance of choosing God to keep us sane and stable as I read the powerful story in Acts 14 about the traveling ministry team of Paul and Barnabas—how without it, they would have surely gone mad. After preaching a strong message, leading people to Christ, these men went from being one moment loved to the next moment hated…adored and revered to running scared for their life.

> Verses 11-18: Paul and Barnabas put on a pedestal and in the spotlight, worshipped by men. Brought flowers and oxen to sacrifice. Thought of as Greek gods.
>
> Verses 19-20: Paul and Barnabas hated, stoned (Paul), and left for dead.

I cannot imagine what this type of emotional gear shifting would have done to the psyche of these men had they not initially made the choice for God. Surely it would have messed them up to go from being wildly popular to nearly being murdered. This hot and cold, loved then hated life would be mentally terrorizing, though these warrior preachers experienced it a lot. Without Jesus grounding them, they would have either become too soft to preach a strong gospel (for fear of losing popularity) or scared to death to make such bold moves.

This is the risk and instability of the flesh life—that in both praise and in hatred, we get lost and fall from the faith. It is why well-meaning pastors, once hungry to preach a strong word, have been swayed to now preach a watered-down gospel in order to stay popular. It is why believers have been scared into staying silent and doing nothing out of fear of the bold faith life. In both of these human rubs there is only one answer: choose God if you want to keep your sanity through it all.

Paul and Barnabas could have gotten lost and jaded and quit. But they set themselves up well so that would not be an option—their focus remained on Jesus and the gospel message carried on with an irrelevance to its reception. If we want to live Jesus strong, we, too, have to operate this way: eyes on God, full steam ahead, the only way of survival for believers in this life. In adulation or rejection, we are able to stay solid in the truth that it's never about us, no matter how it seems.

It's God, always God, only God, forever God. It's looking up, locking eyes with our Master, walking the gospel out. It's putting our warrior boots on and living the choice we already made. When we choose God, we choose sanity. We choose balance. "Always God, only God, forever God" may seem like a simple life mantra and strategy, but it is more than that: it is the choice to combat a reactionary life. Vital things don't become vital in their complication—the most helpful things in life are often simple at their core: sleep enough, eat right, exercise, the end. With God, it's the simple core things too: read your Bible, pray, confess sin, love, and serve, the end.

So we've read all the books and we've never changed? Maybe we haven't yet taken it core and simple. So many things in life are off-kilter when my relationship with God is not good. When we have problems in a home we better be wise enough to look at the structure first to see what we are working with and make sure it's all good—otherwise, no wonder the floors are caving in or there is a crazy leak. It's not the floors. It's not the leak. It's the structure.

In many life instances we battle a misplaced perceived enemy—we are not fighting our inability to set boundaries, in some cases, though that is what at the moment it may seem. That's a symptom of the larger problem. We are battling self, which doesn't know how to get our priorities in order without the help of God. So many smokescreen problems we determine are our core problem—iceberg issues and we deal with just the tip.

> *So many things in life are off-kilter when my relationship with God is not good.*

Friends, when we make a choice for God and do not waver from it, we are surprised by how orderly our life gets. When we choose God, our relationships get much more healthy and stable and it naturally becomes much clearer to us when to say no. When we choose God, it stabilizes our fragile egos to receive praise and respect and not let popularity go to our head. It doesn't mean we don't have complications we need to address or iceberg issues along the way. It just means we have taken care of the real business first so the other things can actually get fixed.

WEEK 6

# I WILL CHOOSE GOD

**Take a Deeper Dive:** Deuteronomy 30

**10 minutes:** Welcome. Share about a recent hard choice you have made (funny or serious).

**10 Minutes:** Intro to chapter through Video Teaching with Lisa (outline and videos available online at www.warriorbootsbook.com)

**35 Minutes:** Small Group Discussion (Take the first 10 minutes to answer privately, then the last 25 to discuss as a group.)

1. "You have to be willing to be alone and separate from the crowd to achieve greatness." What does this mean to you in the context of your spiritual life?

2. Is it possible to live the "solo" life and have a family? Why are these not really at odds?

3. The choice to love, obey, and commit—which do you think believers have the hardest time with?

4. Does the idea of "just the facts" living appeal to you? Why or why not? Can you see the importance of it regardless?

5. Why is outfitting your life to support your choices so necessary?

6. Do you agree that the world lacks both sanity and stability? Why is your choice for God really the choice for these things?

**Prayer:** God, we find ourselves drowning in choices, struggling to make right decisions. Help us to see that the choice for You is the choice to stabilize our life and our mind. We want to live a solo life for You, yet we are pulled in so many directions. Give us clarity and strength; help us outfit our life for the choice of You. Yes and amen.

**Bonus Home Helps:**

1. Do a word study of *choose/choice* from Scripture.

2. Memorize and meditate on Deuteronomy 30:20: "You can make this choice by loving the LORD your God, obeying him, and committing yourself firmly to him. This is the key to your life."

3. Write one sentence in your journal about how well you've loved God this year, obeyed God this year, and committed yourself to God this year. Write a sentence under it in another color ink to say how you want to love, obey, and commit to Him greater right now.

4. Write down one "just the facts" thing about God you need to know right now. Put it on a sticky note and attach to your car dash or mirror or somewhere you see it.

5. Ask someone close to you to pray for you to love, obey, and commit to God greater and live out this four-word (*I Will Choose God*) declaration in your life.

## Journal

# I WILL FOLLOW GOD FOREVER

If the LORD is God, follow him!

**1 KINGS 18:21**

Sometimes compliments unearth hidden insecurities.

Several years ago I am given two gracious compliments that mean much and simultaneously mess me up for a while. I am a human wired for affirmation, but these compliments left me with an unexpected identical sense: the overwhelming desire for the compliment to be true and the horrible feeling someone might have gotten it all wrong.

The first comes from a long-distance friend during a phone conversation, as we talk about remaining a strong Christian witness in the midst of a godless world: "Lisa, I don't believe you will ever leave God. You are one of the faithful God followers."

The second, later and unrelated, from a pastor-friend via e-mail, in a kind gesture of support: "You are always the same person, preaching the same thing. I appreciate the consistency in you."

The friends mean the words to encourage my heart, and they do. They say them to tell me they notice my love for God, and in the depth of my soul, I am grateful. I am a wobbly-kneed, stubborn bull of a woman with rough edges, loads of poor behavior, and a plethora of sins I continue to rack up daily. Jesus is all I've got to show for myself. So to hear these things said by friends in unrelated conversations feels like God and I have gotten somewhere after all these years together, and He's using them to let me know.

But at the same time, in the weeks that follow, they bring out insecurities and a nagging awareness of gaps in my relationship with God. I am consumed by the need to examine them. I want to believe the compliments are true. I want to believe that regardless of anything, I will never leave God, and despite the crazy of this world, I will stay steady and consistent in my faith.

But these are strong claims. This means I live a life of *no matter what*. I know what this could mean, and though I have faced obstacles in my life like everyone else, I haven't faced all the *no matter what's* yet, I am sure. I know too much from watching the lives of my friends, the news, the next-door neighbors where in the lives of good people, things have gone terribly wrong.

This life of *no matter what* means no matter life or death, loss or gain, joy or sorrow, richness or bankruptcy, life's highs and life's desperate lows, when things make sense and when they never can. I stay and I follow a God who both expects and deserves my same level of love and allegiance in both. I can read this in the Bible and nod my head as a yes, but living the realities are different than when they are on paper. Deep down I think these are the fears we all have: that some *no matter what* will come into our life and finally be too much and we will crumple into a ball of anger or pain we cannot continue to love and trust God through. Some of us have already had this tested.

*Jesus is all I've got to show for myself.*

So I sit and I think. Instead of answering in my mind a definitive *I will* to these compliments, I find myself questioning, *Will I?* Will I stay with God forever? Will I consistently follow Him *no matter what*? These questions are important ones we don't often consider. We don't like to plan out our staying strategy with God, and it's one of our biggest mistakes as believers. In so doing, we underestimate the spiritual war. This is the most important journey we will ever go on in our life, the one with the most benefits and repercussions for both now and eternity, the one that affects so many other people, and we decide to wing it. Could it be that we are living a life of roller-coaster spirituality and Kingdom ineffectiveness, all due to poor planning? What a costly mistake to make with a relatively simple fix.

Having a strategy for following God is more important than ever, in these hard and desperate times. It takes absolutely nothing away from a vibrant, free spiritual life to strategize for our spiritual success—in fact, our spiritual health depends upon it. God can work the most organically and powerfully through a vessel that has adequately prepared her life to follow Him. The more we follow God, the more natural it is to follow Him (notice I didn't say easier). If we plant our roots down deep in God, in that grounded space, we can see the spiritual freedom and victory we have always wanted.

> But blessed are those who trust in the LORD
> and have made the LORD their hope and confidence.
> They are like trees planted along a riverbank,
> with roots that reach deep into the water.
> Such trees are not bothered by the heat
> or worried by long months of drought.
> Their leaves stay green,
> and they never stop producing fruit.
> (Jeremiah 17:7-8)

We are planted, we are rooted, we are deep, we aren't bothered, we stay and produce fruit, according to Jeremiah, all because we have *made* the Lord our everything in the midst of the drought. *Made* is an action word on our part; it is something we determine to do. If we want to follow God forever, we have to set it up this way. The good news is, we can.

Will we ever leave God? Not if we plant deep and stay close.

Can we keep following Him forever? Yes, if we daily live our spiritual disciplines.

Not only can we, but we must. In this day and time, it is crucial.

## The Ministry of Sameness

In this crazy and getting crazier world, I've been thinking a lot about what the world really needs from us, the Christians. If we are going to follow God, we are going to have to shift from the mentality that it's just about saving ourselves. Let me be blunt: our careless attitude about the world is sin. This was not the way of our Father then, and not the way of our Father now. His life was about sacrifice, a word we don't fully understand. Following God means following the example of death on a cross. This is an epic task for human beings, but we can humanly emulate it or He wouldn't have given us the charge of Matthew 16:24—to "take up your cross, and follow me."

We live real, ordinary lives and do everyday things. But picking up our cross daily doesn't look like living our life just to go to the gym so we can impress people with our bodies. It doesn't look like Facebook for hours and manic holiday or vacation planning, from one trip to the next. Most of us treat our daily life like a shopping spree of personal indulgence with a few token purchases of the Great Commission thrown in. Our flesh is at constant odds with the life we are called to live, and this is what causes us angst. Why are so many of us chronically unhappy, even when we have so much? We weren't created to live the life that serves ourselves. The shoe never fits. Our life goals have to change, or we will never truly find joy.

We follow God to obey Him, to help ourselves live well, and to give the world what it needs from us. It is a three-fold commitment until the moment of Christ's return, and only our choice to follow God makes it possible.

I suspect that the world doesn't need more of our Christianese language to help it, certainly not the hollow words. We've said a bunch and most of it is not wildly productive. I know we mean well in this. We want to say something to fill the awkward spaces and offer something in moments that feel helpless. We know we are meant to be the mouthpieces for peace, for joy, for love…so we try to fill that role with pat answers and prerecorded messages. But in so many cases, our words lack the Holy Spirit power behind them to help.

When something bad happens in the world, it's our tendency to try to make it better by handing over our best words. And yes, we must preach the gospel, and yes, we must testify to the saving, changing work of the Lord in our own lives so the world will know what they can have. But words alone are not what the world needs to turn to Christ. We've tried this kind of speech giving. Only the words from the Word have the power not to return void, so let us use them the very most.

What the world needs from us is *a steadfast life*: preaching the same, loving the same, doing the same, being the same, no matter what. *A ministry of sameness. The gift of stability.*

And it's not just the unbelievers who need it. We, the Jesus followers, need the ministry of strength and sameness from each other, too, as the body of Christ is greatly encouraged when, despite our struggles, we see each other maintain a steadfast faith in God. It is as Paul writes to the Thessalonians to say in his beautifully brotherly way, *let me encourage you as you have encouraged us* (speaking of Timothy, his mentee and colaborer in Christ). "It gives us new life, knowing you remain strong in the Lord" (1 Thessalonians 3:8 NLT). Jesus followers are buoyed in faith by one who remains.

How rare is this commodity, in this day and time, with all the flux and instability, and how welcomed is a strong, anchored life. We are largely missing this piece as believers to a lost and dying world with the gaping need to be grounded. You can see our need for this anchoring in all our trying for the next best thing to bring us happiness—we will literally try anything to keep us from floating around without course. We long for everlasting hope, fulfillment, and love like an elusive lover. This is a good longing, a Jesus longing, the longing that must happen to save our lives. The breakdown is in the way we try to satisfy it, not in the longing itself. Nothing but God ever anchors us, and many people don't want to try Him. So loads of us stay in deep water and either eventually drown or just keep drifting.

We offer people the ministry of sameness, though they may not know it is even what they need. Yet ask any of us—among the most treasured things we have in life are people whom we know we can count on to be there for us, most of us only being able to identify a precious few. There is something that brings comfort to humans when we know what to expect from someone and where we will find them.

I don't remember many details from my past, but I remember the consistent smell of acrylic paints in my grandmother's art room always in the same spots on the counter, whose familiarity made me feel safe...the reassuring, stable presence of my mother's voice when I call her with something wrong, even to this day...the predictability of my favorite deacon at church as I was growing up who would always smile at me the same way, in the same place every Sunday.

These same things time and again brought me comfort and let me know my world was okay. Even now, years and churches later, I have my church favorite and his name is Randy, a smiley man with snow-white beard and hair. Randy doesn't know it, but I count on him to be at church, smiling. I count on him to hug my kids and tell them how much he loves them. Randy is consistent, and we can all count on him, even though Randy has faced some of the hardest of life himself. I hope he never stops showing up. He has no idea how many rough Sunday mornings in the car have been washed away by 30 seconds of Randy's ministry of sameness.

*The ministry of sameness is not about the unwillingness to grow; it is about being a solid, consistent person to count on.*

This is it, friends. This is the missing piece. We've got to be able to be counted on, and right now, most of us are not because of all of our own entanglements, fear issues, and hurrying. How many things could be washed away in the hurting hearts of people were we to offer them the ministry of sameness? They would know where to find us when they were in pain. They would know what message we would be preaching. They would know where to go for a voice of reason when something happens in this world and know what voice they can respect to be loving, balanced, and stable. Right now they don't know where to look. Too many times we wreck our witness by our lack of credibility and miss the opportunity to serve God.

Instead of looking to jump on social justice bandwagons to validate our spiritual life in public, perhaps we instead should start privately praying that God will help us live a spiritually consistent life. The mark of walking strong and following Jesus will be in the manifestation of our mature consistency. It's our only shot to help this world.

*The ministry of sameness* is not about the unwillingness to grow; it is about being a solid, consistent person to count on. It is showing up for people in the place they know us to be, preaching the same message with our hearts and hands and life. People should expect us to be crying over orphans and taking them into our home. It should come as no surprise when we do. They should expect us to be preaching the singular message that Jesus is the only way. They should expect us to be the first to help the hurting and calming the world's tensions and wisely giving counsel in a turned-around world and loving hard and strong while other people are living reckless and cold.

Consistency is what the world craves; consistency is what we all need—to be known by our sameness: the ones to love and the ones to live holy and the ones to stay faithful to Jesus, no matter what. Our life needs to say, *You know where to find me. This is where I am and where I'll always be—this is where you can find me at any time, on any given day. You can count on my consistency.* People will know they can count on Jesus by how consistently His followers live.

- **A consistent person will be sure.** Sure of what we believe. Sure of what we know about God. Sure and unwavering. Most people aren't sure about anything, so we have to be different.

- **A consistent person will be tireless.** Yes, we are human. When we try to lead from our flesh, we will become exhausted. But when we lead in the Spirit, we are replenished, consistently. (At the same time, do not neglect biblical rest. There must be wisdom in the balance.)

- **A consistent person will be specific.** We can't beat around the bush, be passive-aggressive with our faith. The world needs clear direction and teaching—for us to be specific about what to do and how to survive unstable times.

- **A consistent person will be selfless.** We can't do this life thing if we are not, because eventually, selfish people can't maintain a servant lifestyle—we will only manage short bursts of benevolence. It's not about us. It's not about our words. It's not even about our story, for the sake of telling people about our life. It's not about popularity. It's not about followers and being accepted. It's not about getting things off our chest, pontificating our opinions, writing and speaking for a particular response. It's about being strong and wise. It's about just being about God.

In story after story I read recently about viewpoints and convictions changing to match society and I hear about hard, hurtful things that happen all across this world...I realize, anew, the importance of

being where we are supposed to be and preaching what we are supposed to preach. A perfect God designed a timeless solution with
the gospel. When it comes to this life, there is a one-size-fits-all message to preach: Jesus is the only answer. I fear some of us are veer-
ing from this out of our own numbness to truth, culture's pressure,
and the humanistic message that we can create our own solutions.
There's nothing redundant or boring about preaching the message
that answers every question, resolves every area of need. What other
message do we preach that can untangle such complicated issues?
What other message can reach across vast conflict and form a bridge?
What other message is big enough to silence the white noise of world
confusion and turmoil? No, this message must never get old. Jesus is
the only One to solve all the many things, and this will never change.

If we are to follow Jesus and walk strong in warrior boots, we are
going to have to resolve some things in our own heart first. If we are
to offer to this world the ministry of sameness, we are going to need
to answer these three questions for ourselves:

1. **Where will I be so they can find me?** This is not about
   location. This is about someone being able to know they
   can reach out to you in their moment of trouble, and
   you will be found consistently being the person they
   always knew you to be.

2. **What will I be preaching?** In other words, what will
   your main message you offer to people, especially in this
   hard time, be? What message are you known for and
   how does it point people to God?

3. **What will they be able to count on me for?** Will you
   provide the strength, hope, joy, and stability to people
   that, as a representative of Jesus, people can and even
   should expect? It's not about being perfect, on, or never
   having a bad day. It's about consistently exercising the
   fruit of the Spirit.

When we know the answers to these questions, the other people will start to know too.

---

*A perfect God designed a timeless
solution with the gospel.*

---

## Following

I read something today that gave me pause, which I admit is happening more and more often.

It's from a spiritual leader I know (and genuinely like) only from afar but often disagree with theologically. At first, his words sound really good. He says that those who are hurt often turn into healers. My heart swells at this thought of goodness coming from pain. I like the sound of this. It feels strong and good.

But then I remember that sometimes good-sounding things aren't completely true (i.e., "time heals all wounds"), and no one actually has the ability to heal but God. It's practical and rains on the feelings parade, I know. But it's true. We who get hurt in life can become leaders in the healing ministry but only *with and through the power of God.* Leaving that part out may make for better quotable sentences that pull on our heartstrings. But when we leave out God in any equation, there's a problem. It's one of the most effective and backhanded ways Satan confuses us away from the real Help.

We have to become wiser about whom we follow. Self-help talk that sounds good but isn't exactly true is becoming more and more the encouragement of choice in this society. I read these kinds of things every day—how we can heal ourselves, be our own one true love, create our own purpose for the future…how we are enough, in and of ourselves, and we have greatness and power inside ourselves to do the job. And I just want to weep because I know these things that are close are moving us farther from Jesus. We keep hearing these messages, and moving away from the gospel. It doesn't matter how good they sound. Good without God is void of power.

We aren't enough. It's not true that we are. Only God is enough, and we aren't a close second.

We aren't the healers; we are the helpers. We help point people in the direction of where to be healed.

We aren't the ones who know what to do, we are the ones who preach about the only One who does.

Close is one of Satan's favorite deceptive tools.

Because close still keeps us from God but is often hard to detect. Close is not healing. Close is not love. Close is not salvation. When Paul, arrested by the Romans on his third missionary journey for preaching the gospel, appeared to King Agrippa in court to speak in his defense and told his powerful story of conversion by God on the road to Damascus, King Agrippa said to him these words: "You almost persuade me to become a Christian" (Acts 26:28 NKJV).

Almost. Close. But still not. People have died and missed heaven over being close. People have lived their whole life saying they might turn to God. We give people mixed signals when we, the believers in Jesus Christ, offer them alternatives for face on the floor, contrite heart, total submission to God, the very thing that will save them.

---

*Good without God is void of power.*

---

Jesus gave us the heads-up that in this day and time there would be people close but still far who even worship the things He Himself has made but completely overlook Him. I heard this very thing come true today while watching an interview on TV with a woman with Corvette-red hair who said about her religious preferences: "I'm actually just spiritual. I believe in the stars and the moon and the sun and the trees and all of nature." And I remembered the passage in Romans where it says, "So they worshiped and served the things

God created instead of the Creator himself, who is worthy of eternal praise! Amen "(1:25). He said it would happen, and it does and did.

The answer to all of this is not offering more creative ways to help people in this world feel good and strong; it is to effectively persuade them to follow God. People will never come to God if we keep telling them they can do it all themselves. This will be on our hands, the ones who know the truth but settled on something close. We already know that it is in the leadership He provides that we find strength like never before, a steadiness, a fulfillment, and life determination. It's Him who brings the hope and the calm to our chaos. We don't need to try to come up with new solutions; we need to help people find God. The danger in following a message or messenger who promotes one's own answers as the way to life fulfillment can't be overstated. In this dark and stormy time, the accountability we are held to as both the receiver and giver of any message is high. Following God is our only hope. Any other message is futile.

Following God is not our natural tendency, even if our personality is one that more naturally follows the crowd. Because our flesh fights us, it's not easy to hand over the map to Him and let Him drive without our input. So many of us say we will follow God or we do follow God, but often it is laced with contingency plans and places to bail out. When God tells us to follow Him, He means all in, giving up all control. Only He knows the way, so this completely makes sense. We just aren't great followers much of the time. So the last thing we need is falsely believing we share the compass.

**Following means resolution to be behind.** There is no side-by-side relationship when it comes to God. We are with Him and He is with us, but He's in the leadership role. (Remember the parenting style I mentioned? A balance of human respect and natural hierarchy.) Yes, we have friendship, and God treats us with love and honor. So much so that He lets us rest from the burden of knowing where we are going. Yet another way our God is gracious.

**Following means we are sure of the person up ahead.** We have to be surer of God, our leader, than we are of ourselves. The human tendency is to trust in our own flesh when we have never proven to be capable of such trust in the past. We need not be sure of anything or anyone else.

**Following means we give up the right to know the way.** When we gave our lives to God we committed ourselves to this. Fear and doubt keep telling us to take the control back. God didn't get any less capable; we just started giving into our flesh.

**Following means we stay close.** God's pace is never careless. He doesn't go too fast or too slow or take a road we aren't able to travel. We're the ones who take detours, hesitate, wander off, pull over to the side, and quit. We aren't very good followers many times because we have let too much space get between us and God and that allows in outside influence. Only when we are fastened securely and safely to Him will we keep the perfect pace.

I wake one night not long ago with the word *tethered* on my brain, without cause. Immediately, my mind races back to sixth grade and the Missouri sun shining down on our favorite recess game of tetherball. I was never very good at it, to be honest, but some of my classmates were. How well I can remember how they would ball up their fist and swing their arm, hitting that volleyball on a string around that metal pole, wrapping itself again and again and again. I remember the ball on that rope, fastened tight to that pole, and I remember thinking as a kid that if it weren't, it would surely fly off into oblivion.

Fascinated by the random memory, I look up the definition of *tether* and read, "A rope, chain, or the like, by which an animal is fastened to a fixed object so as to limit its range of movement." About the same time as tetherball, we lived out on some land where my family kept horses, and we would tether them to the fence so they wouldn't get away, though at the time I just called it tying them up. The horses never got away, in all those years we had them. Perhaps we had them so well tethered.

Today, without being tethered so closely to God, none of us will make it. The world is hitting us so hard, my friends, that without being fastened tightly we will surely fly away. It's not just about saying we will follow God; it's about allowing ourselves to be tethered to God so that we are actually able to follow through with it. Our good intentions to follow aren't enough. Walking behind but not staying close isn't an option. Being fringe but not center won't work. We won't ever truly be able to follow God long term if we let slack come into our rope. Our relationship was meant to be tighter than that.

> *People will never come to God if we keep telling them they can do it all themselves.*

Missionary Elisabeth Elliot said it beautifully: "Where does your security lie? Is God your refuge, your hiding place, your stronghold, your shepherd, your counselor, your friend, your redeemer, your Saviour, your guide? If He is, you don't need to search any further for security." Being tethered tightly to God is the only secure thing.

If we are going to put our warrior boots on and walk Jesus strong, we are going to have to stop offering alternative ways to ourselves and others to find the stable and fulfilling life we so desperately want. Close will not cut it. Almost is not enough. We are going to have to resolve that we will always be behind, are sure of the Person leading us, are willing to give up the right to know the way, and will tether ourselves to God so tightly nothing can come between us. For the believer in Jesus it will all come down to this: if the Lord is God, follow Him.

## Spoken Hope

If following God is our choice, then so is living a life of hope. Because the only way to ever truly have hope is to have it in the Hope that will not disappoint (Romans 5:5).

Following God is not for God's sake. Yes, we follow God in

obedience and to offer the world stability in a world that is desperately devoid of it, but we also follow God because without Him, we can't look forward to our future. The best choice I have ever made is to follow a God I can't see but can fully trust. It's lunacy to a lost world but makes perfect sense in life. No one can argue personal testimony—how in my own life, following Jesus has made me live without losing my sanity—the same is true for you as a Jesus follower, I feel sure. All I know is that every day I live on earth is too hard for a pep talk. I can't just tell myself tomorrow will be better because I don't honestly know. There is no hope for me without God. Him inside of us rallies the darkest of places to a hopeful place again. I need His hope every hour of every day or I can't make it.

We've already discussed how we can't save ourselves, heal ourselves, be our own healer or life giver, so that is without question. We also can't rally ourselves into hope, no matter what the world tells us. But our practical God has done something unique and special for us to help ourselves in a tangible way: He created us with senses to follow up on His good work inside. We use our legs to go physically into a church when we need community, our hands to serve the poor. We close our eyes when we need rest. We open our mouth when our body needs nourishment. God is such a pragmatist that He left no detail out for how we would thrive best in this world.

Following God means we utilize every part of ourselves to honor Him. It's not just our mind and our heart, but also our body. Everything must be engaged for His leadership in us to work. Hope honors Him. So do peace and strength. Purity honors Him. Discipline and right living do too. The mind is a powerful tool for either helping or hurting, and so are the eyes and ears and lips. What we take in is of huge importance; what we put out is too. So it makes sense that the things we say to ourselves either support our following God and His good work in us or hinder it. This is not us being our own saviors. It is us letting the greatest Life Coach coach us through words of hope from His heart to our lips.

*Have you ever spoken hope to yourself?*

This may sound like some new age process, but I assure you, with God at the center, it is not. It's actually something powerful David did in his life, to utilize his mouth to speak words to his heart to help his spirit rally, a soul declaration. This powerful process of speaking scripture to ourselves, speaking hope, keeps us on the straight path of following God despite the pressure of this world. It was a regular practice for David, and three times within a span of 11 verses in Psalm 42 and 43 (NKJV) he spoke hope to himself:

- Psalm 42:5: "Why are you cast down, O my soul? And why are you disquieted within me? Hope in God, for I shall yet praise Him for the help of His countenance."

- Verse 11: "Why are you cast down, O my soul? And why are you disquieted within me? Hope in God; for I shall yet praise Him, the help of my countenance and my God."

- Psalm 43:5: "Why are you cast down, O my soul? And why are you disquieted within me? Hope in God; for I shall yet praise Him, the help of my countenance and my God."

Three times he uses the same words. Three times he asks himself the hard question and then speaks the answer out loud. It is always in praising God we find strength and power. It is always in declaring truth and acknowledging He alone is our help we have hope. It is not about what we feel; it is about what we know. God won't disappoint us, and He's the only One who won't. He has given us a mouth by which to confess this greatness, at times to others and sometimes to ourselves—life declarations, just like the chapter declarations in this book. When we commit to follow God, we seal the sacred promise of hope. The world is loud, and sometimes the only way to quiet it is to speak over it. Spoken hope is a gift God has given us from the Word to our own lips, straight to our heart. It's one of the best tools He has given us to keep following hard after Him.

### Going Back to the Solid Place

I write this chapter in the weeks following the killing of some black men by police officers and subsequent retaliation against the police—what's becoming a continued thread as I'm writing this book in what seems the constant chaos of this world. There's been a lot of killing on the news lately, too much horrific killing, and I'm praying that by the time this book comes out this violence will have stopped. But I know the nature of this world in turmoil, and I know that unless there is a corporate turning back to God, there will be more of this and other heinous things we do not yet know. It grieves me to see our world this way, and yet I know without such desperation our stubborn hearts will never bow in submission to God. Our hearts are at war, and it's showing up in our behavior.

The reality is that everything imperfect, wrong, horrible, unfulfilling, and seemingly hopeless drives us to God for this reason: there is no other answer. This is the best worst reality of our life. God is our stable place, but most of us have to stumble and limp our way over to Him. It's not the way He wants it, but He knows it is the way of our choosing. It is a blessed thing to be in a no-way-out position: the Savior is the only One there.

My friend Sarah was going through one of the hardest times of her life last year, and in the midst of her struggle she tells me she is reading this book and I should read it too: *The Inner Voice of Love* by Henri Nouwen. He writes it when he's in a mental institution, the mask is off, and he can no longer pretend he's not a wreck. It's a secret journal of sorts, and published years later after some heavy prompting from friends. Sarah needed the words, she tells me, because her life is a wreck too. She's forgotten who she is and if she can truly be loved. The pages become a healing friend.

I pick up the book and start to read, since I am an endless well of neediness of God's love and attention myself. I come to an entry called "Always Come Back to the Solid Place," and though that is only the title, it is the entire message I need to hear. I know what this means, to always come back to the solid place. I recognize the language of the wanderer. In my own life, I have had to come back to God many times because I left. *I left.* It's lunacy to walk away from something so good. To leave a God so powerful and loving seems like insanity, and this is indeed where the residual insanities start. When we leave God, we start marching the death march and eventually we reach the end: the end of ourselves, the end of goodness, the end of our standards, the end of peace, the end of the hopeful life. Getting to go back is God's grace, not our brilliance.

Nouwen knew of this grace, Sarah knows of it, and so do I. None of us can claim we have never wandered or we would be divinity. To what degree we wander about or outright leave in a fit of rebellious rage makes no difference. It is the going back that is important.

"You have to trust the place that is solid…you have to choose the solid place over and over again and return to it after every failure."[1] *Trust. Choose. Return.* These are good, true words. Most of us are in one of these spaces right this very moment. We are in need of trust. We need to choose. We need to return. Following God cannot be done without trust; it cannot be done without choosing to let Him lead; it cannot be done if we do not return to Him after the leaving.

My friend, you may be in the darkest hole of your life right now. You may be a complete wreck, and no one would touch you with a ten-foot pole if they could see inside your heart. But you aren't too scary for God. Your wanderings are not a surprise, and it's not the first time He's been left. But if you're going to be able to walk strong in this world, you're going to have to come back to the solid place. Those warrior boots will walk differently on solid ground. One of the most comforting things about a following-God journey is that you release the pressure to believe in yourself. You don't have to do this; you don't have to trust people you cannot trust, even yourself.

You don't have to trust the process; you just have to trust God in the process. Knowing this makes all the difference in the way we walk in this world.

---

*You aren't too scary for God.*

---

A favorite song by Christy Nockels reminds me of this stabilizing solid place: "Find me at the feet of Jesus." I listen to this song over and over again, every time I speak, because it reminds me that to be sane I must stay at His feet. My flesh makes me forget my location, more than I wish were true. The feet of Jesus, oh yes, that's where I am to be...the solid place. This is where I need to be for me and where people need to know I'll be. We can't mess up at the feet of Jesus. Most of us have just gotten up and are not where we are supposed to be, so it's no wonder life went off the rails. Following God is a constant coming back with the goal of staying in the solid place at His feet.

A strong warrior for God will be determined by the depth and consistency of our following. We can leave Him, but every time we do, we weaken ourselves. Equally beautiful to a story of God's radical work in a wanderer's life is the story of a gray-haired Jesus follower who has loved and followed Him for a long time, though we don't always honor it like we should. Longevity with God is not a boring, predictable story. It is not lived by a person who has never experienced the world. None of us are immune to the temptations and hardships of a broken world. But we who choose to follow God and love Him, long time, are the ones with the greatest benefit of His character because we have chosen to have more of Him. We can tell those whom He has rubbed off on the most, I think.

Following God over time creates history and builds up a strong reserve. God doesn't tell us to follow Him because He's on some ego trip; He tells us to follow Him because He knows the way. When we learn to follow God and say yes to Him, over and over again, we become warriors. It's not enough to say we want God or know we need God; it's a choice to radically follow Him. A choice to keep pursuing, though we are a haggard mess. The choice to stay faithful even when everyone around is faithless. To choose God when other things beg for our attention and priority.

Because in the end, it will be the relationship built on history of God's personal faithfulness to us that readies us to be warriors.

If the Lord is your God, follow Him, friends.

Follow Him hard. Follow Him only. Follow Him, forever.

# I WILL FOLLOW GOD FOREVER

**Take a Deeper Dive:** Jeremiah 17:7-8

**10 minutes:** Welcome. Share about a time you followed God, regardless of feelings or knowledge of outcome.

**10 Minutes:** Intro to chapter through Video Teaching with Lisa (outline and videos available online at www.warriorbootsbook.com)

**35 Minutes:** Small Group Discussion (Take the first 10 minutes to answer privately, then the last 25 to discuss as a group.)

1. Is it possible, in this day and time, to have a stable and thriving Christian life and stay off the spiritual roller coaster? Why do you think many believers don't?

2. What does the ministry of sameness mean to you? How has consistency of a person/persons in your life helped you on your journey?

3. What does following God look like?

4. Do you believe the habit of spoken hope is important? Why or why not?

5. What do you the words "going back to the solid place" mean to you?

**Prayer:** God, we want to follow You with our whole lives and hearts. We want to stop questioning You at every turn and get off the spiritual roller coaster. We confess that we haven't trusted You enough, and You are trustworthy. Help us live a life of sameness and consistency. Help us speak the hope from Your Word to ourselves. Thank

You for being the solid place we can go back to again and again, no matter what. Yes and amen.

**Bonus Home Helps:**

1. Do a word study of *follow* from Scripture.

2. Memorize and meditate on 1 Kings 18:21: "If the LORD is God, follow him!"

3. Write down these three questions and spend time praying over them and then finally answering them on paper: *Where will I be so they can find me?* (Think about your schedule. Can people get ahold of you in need, or are you always too busy? Where could someone find you if they went looking—on Sunday at church? In your neighborhood, talking to neighbors? Or in your house, out shopping, etc.?) *What will I be preaching?* (Think about what specific message your life/experience/gifts God can use and what ministry moves your heart the most.) *What will they be able to count on me for?* (What do people say about you—that you are the loving one, the serving one, the bold one, the consistent one? This gives you insight into what people count on you to provide.)

4. Make a timeline of your life up until now. Write down ages, important dates, crucial life moments. (However you want to do it and is easiest for you to recall.) Make a little jot mark in yellow of all the places/times you've gone back to the solid place of God after a hard time or a time you walked away from the Lord that you can remember. Thank Him for being there and being ever consistent in your life.

5. Ask someone close to you to pray for you to trust God greater and live out this five-word (*I Will Follow God Forever*) declaration in your life.

## Journal

# I AM READY

Though this world, with devils filled, should
threaten to undo us; we will not fear, for God
hath willed His truth to triumph through us.
**MARTIN LUTHER**

I've only watched two people die. The first was my grandmother, who took her very last breath while I was in the room. It was a holy experience, I'll tell you. I knew with her last gasp of air that she was with her Jesus. I saw that eternal moment for myself on this side, feeling like a voyeur to destiny, and it forever changed how I pictured my own mortality.

The second person is my father. This is a little different. I've been watching him die for months, slipping away every day. By the time this book is published he will likely be with his Jesus, and I'm hoping I'll be far enough past the tears to smile again. In my quiet moments, my mind conjures pictures for the words I don't have—my daddy drowning deeper and deeper, and I can't quite grab his arm to pull him out. He has a progressive palsy, a rare central nervous system disease which takes his life slowly and virtually painlessly—which I know is a great gift. But it doesn't feel like a gift when my strong hero lies in a bed with hair he cannot comb and sunshine on his face he cannot feel. Every day I can't be with him I ask my mother how much more he has died today. One day I know the answer will be, "He's all the way gone."

I've never done life without my father. I know many people have, so to be 45 with this complaint feels small to some. But to me, it is an experience tied into my confidence level, my entire life history, who I am and who I was and who I can be, for my father has always been my biggest cheerleader. I don't want my cheerleader to go to heaven. I don't want my strong father to be weak—because what would that mean for his daughter, who is cut from his same cloth? I can't pretend anymore. Even the strongest of humans cannot defy the cycle of life.

In my fragile state, I am especially grateful right now to remember how ultimately my strength comes from Jesus and that my feelings are not what determines my readiness, yes, even after the sting of death. I have faced other hardships this year—taking my first-born to college, two unplanned moves, some health concerns of my own—and I anticipate other hard things to come because I anticipate *life*. All of us share this uncertainty of a residence that is not heaven. All of us have to deal with our own hard. And all of us have to make this warrior boots declaration *I am ready* based on our faith and trust in God, not on the circumstances and how we may feel. My friends, we can do this. Not only can we—we must.

We're doing great things, you and me. Doing hard things. Doing things we aren't proud of (and some we really, really are).

We're loving people well and sometimes treating people *less than*. Losing our temper, forgetting to take hold of the battle for our mind and watching it slip from us. We're making progress and then falling back and feeling worse. We're crazy broken every day, but still holding on to hope in our core because *Jesus*.

We're eating food that makes us happy and carrying the weight that makes us sad. We're finding community over the table, which is the forgotten best thing, and *oh, those consuming cell phones*. We have pets we love and gardens we tend and places we drive and meals we cook and laundry we wash and schools and jobs we go to.

We have private pains in our hearts over loves who've gone to heaven and people who hurt us here on earth. We have broken relationships and friends who *get it* and send the text just in time.

We're doing well with God and then before we mean to, leaving God out of things completely. Praying like mad or going days without prayer at all. We have worries, so many, even when we know we shouldn't. We have bursts of faith that surprise us.

We have weak bodies, strong bodies, old bodies we don't recognize anymore. We're winning things, losing things, holding on to things too long, and letting go of things too soon. We're crying because we are sad, crying because something turned out better than we hoped.

This is the life we live now.

One day we will start our real best life and all get better.

My friends, sorting through this hard and beautiful and imperfect life means we are human and we are not yet with Jesus. It doesn't mean we aren't ready to walk Jesus strong, despite the world's mess. For the believer in Jesus Christ, we *are* ready, right now, through the imperfect, despite ourselves. Now is the time to lace up the boots and walk strong. We have important things to get done.

This is really the deal of life: not feeling ready but choosing to walk anyway; important things needing to get done that will require us going ahead by the power of God. As believers in Christ, it is how our whole life will be. So the good news is we can stop wasting time wishing for the magical moment we feel ready to take life on—to put on the warrior boots and walk strong. Life with the reality that our feelings never dictate what we do is a foreign concept to most of us, but it's the way of holy release.

Jesus never asks us to *feel* ready; He asks us to *be* ready. His way is readiness of the mind, heart, and soul. We may be in a wheelchair or have the strongest body of anyone we know: the inner soul is what must be strong. Strong warriors for God are made from holiness and righteousness, not muscle and willpower. So His call on us to be ready is an even playing field for all.

I don't know the circumstances in your life that make you feel not ready. I suspect they are truly hard, likely some harder than mine. I won't pretend to have the pat answer to help your particular heart pain feel better—there are things so dark and hard in this world that only God knows the depth. I won't throw out Christian clichés and ask you to just trust God because it sounds good. I ask you to trust God because there is no other option.

What I can tell you today is that our circumstances do not need to be made right for us to walk this life out strong. We don't need to understand them or make them make sense. Most of us have tried this route and wound up in exhaustion. We don't need to brave ourselves into ready because brave is off the table. We just have to make the decision right now that walking Jesus strong in warrior boots is what we want and living the life declarations we've talked about is what we will do. We need no other information to make this decision than what we already know.

> *Jesus never asks us to feel ready;*
> *He asks us to be ready.*

Because of Jesus, no matter what, you've got this…I've got this… even when we feel like we don't. Even in our weakness, there is work to be done. We are ready to walk in warrior boots because we choose to walk this life out strong. We determine in our hearts that it will not be about the circumstances, but the commitments. These are things a health crisis cannot change. These are things even the deepest, darkest of loss cannot take from us. These are things by the help of the Holy Spirit we can fully be and do.

I'm praying for you today, that Jesus will come near—that He will persuade you by the power of the Holy Spirit that He has created you to walk strong, once and for all. I believe this, to my core. You aren't ready for this and neither am I, but *we are*. Not because we have rallied ourselves to death or taken the "how to survive hard things" class at church or even because we have read this book. Because God. Because the Bible, which is everything we need for life and godliness. Everything. *Every thing.* God knew your hard last year. He knew your dark hole. He knew you could walk strong anyway.

I've talked to us bluntly in this book because hard times call for strong words. If we try to be warriors in this world with soft half-truths and self-appeasing, we try to empty the ocean with a plastic spoon. It's too tough out there, friends. We are created for better than that. It might be hard to hear, but reality is harder to live without full knowledge of survival. Life won't change because we choose not to hear and see it. So we can either be ready for it, or not. Being ready won't mean the next hard thing will be within our ability to manage—it will mean that no matter what that next hard thing is, God will help us through. We don't have to know the particular storm when we know the vehicle to survive. Jesus is our survival, our breath. Without Him, we drown for real or drown and keep living without a pulse.

So then, what to do in our limited, don't feel ready life? Go on anyway. Look at God anyway. Don't feel; believe.

> We determine in our hearts that it will not be
> about the circumstances, but the commitments.

## Promises and Instructions

Clear-cut instructions speak to the bottom-line, simple person in me. Just tell it to me plain. There's a lot of noise out there and in my head, so if you're going to tell me something else, please make the message clear.

Last year I got an office chair I loved but had to put it together myself, and the assembly was possible only because there were four pieces and clear directions (since I am the least assembly-required handy person ever). You should have seen me after it was done, standing back all proudly looking at the white rolling chair of goodness that had come together by the work of my hands, all four pieces of it. No one would have guessed the assembly was simple. It didn't make it any less beautiful; it made it something I could actually do. If it had been complicated, I never would have been able to get the job done.

Kind, gracious, all-knowing Jesus was so good to us when He gave us the instruction of Scripture because He knew too many complex directions would be a problem, at least for people like me. I write books and I went to seminary (full disclosure: I'm a dropout), but I am not a studied theologian. I am an everyday woman who has personally read and learned from smarter people and who has read and studied God's Word.

The Bible is simultaneously as deep as the deepest well and as accessible as the nearest bucket. I never go to it and wind up feeling let down—as many times as I have read its every word, I know I am but on the surface of the deepest of truths to come back to and dive into, more and more. The Bible is the most beautiful because it is written by the divine in a language the human can understand. Only God could pull off such a thing. Wave after wave, truth after truth, depth after depth, the Holy Bible.

In this day and time and in every day and time, the Bible is the answer to life's turbulence. In every book therein, there is a solution to the problems of this world. (What other book can promise that?) In this particular moment it is 1 Peter that I read, and right off the bat, my Bible commentary tells me the *why* behind it:

> The apostle Peter wrote this letter to encourage believers who would likely face trials and persecution under Emperor Nero. During most of the first century, Christians were not hunted down and killed throughout the Roman Empire. They could, however, expect social and economic persecution from three main sources: the

Romans, the Jews, and their own families. All would very likely be misunderstood; some would be harassed; a few would be tortured and even put to death.[1]

This is all very familiar—the trials and persecutions, small compared to death, but trials still—it is the world in which believers now live. In the West, we aren't hunted down and killed for our faith at this point, at least not many of us. (I strongly believe it could be coming.) But when we stand up for God, we are often at the very least misunderstood. Conviction is not popular, and the human mouthpiece by which God uses to deliver it sometimes is the easiest target to dismiss or be angry against. Listen, we must be responsible with the call to call out, if that is indeed what God is asking of us, and the call to live out, which is a constant. We should quiver at the very thought of ever calling out or living out, out of turn or from a place of pride. But telling people not to judge to stop conversations is something we need to get past as believers. It's easy and a typical response, but it stifles needed repentance. Personally, I don't want to get in the way of God in either case.

First Peter 1 was for the believers then, and the believers now. (I know this passage is long, but trust me, it's worth reading every word.)

> This letter is from Peter, an apostle of Jesus Christ.
>
> I am writing to God's chosen people who are living as foreigners in the provinces of Pontus, Galatia, Cappadocia, Asia, and Bithynia. God the Father knew you and chose you long ago, and his Spirit has made you holy. As a result, you have obeyed him and have been cleansed by the blood of Jesus Christ.
>
> May God give you more and more grace and peace.
>
> All praise to God, the Father of our Lord Jesus Christ. It is by his great mercy that we have been born again, because God raised Jesus Christ from the dead. Now we live with great expectation, and we have a priceless inheritance—an

inheritance that is kept in heaven for you, pure and unde-filed, beyond the reach of change and decay. And through your faith, God is protecting you by his power until you receive this salvation, which is ready to be revealed on the last day for all to see.

So be truly glad. There is wonderful joy ahead, even though you have to endure many trials for a little while. These trials will show that your faith is genuine. It is being tested as fire tests and purifies gold—though your faith is far more precious than mere gold. So when your faith remains strong through many trials, it will bring you much praise and glory and honor on the day when Jesus Christ is revealed to the whole world.

You love him even though you have never seen him. Though you do not see him now, you trust him; and you rejoice with a glorious, inexpressible joy. The reward for trusting him will be the salvation of your souls.

This salvation was something even the prophets wanted to know more about when they prophesied about this gracious salvation prepared for you. They wondered what time or situation the Spirit of Christ within them was talking about when he told them in advance about Christ's suffering and his great glory afterward.

They were told that their messages were not for them-selves, but for you. And now this Good News has been announced to you by those who preached in the power of the Holy Spirit sent from heaven. It is all so wonder-ful that even the angels are eagerly watching these things happen (verses 1-12).

Though this whole passage is amazing, these are the things that to me stand out.

1. "God the Father...**chose you long ago**, and his Spirit has made you holy" (verse 2). (Think about it now,

please. God has been loving you for a long time, longer than anyone else. Too incredible for words.)

2. "Now we live with **great expectation**" (verse 3). ("Great expectation" has a nice ring to it, does it not?)

3. "We have a **priceless inheritance**" (verse 4). (Hear this, friend? Good things are ours in the future for sure and for real.)

4. That inheritance "is kept in heaven for you, pure and undefiled, **beyond the reach of change and decay**" (verse 4). (Nothing can touch what God has for you.)

5. "God **is protecting you** by his power until you receive this salvation" (verse 5). (Covering by the Almighty, friends. *Covering.* What's assumed here is your trust in God.)

6. "Though you do not see him now, you trust him [those words, again]; and you rejoice with a **glorious, inexpressible joy**" (verse 8). (So God confirms it: joy on this earth is a real thing.)

Chosen. Wonderful expectation. Priceless inheritance. Beyond the reach of change and decay. Protection. Glorious, inexpressible joy on this earth. How good are these promises? As good as it gets. God offers us these promises, not in a perfect world, but in a messed-up one. Surely He knew our world would be dangerous. Surely He knew about the political fighting and moral decline and human corruption. Surely He knew of our personal horrors and crises. And yet He promises: life is beautiful because He through us overcomes.

I need the promises of God. I count on them to never let me down like human promises. You need them too. We can't be warriors if we don't trust the Strong One and everything He says. If we are having a hard time in this world, perhaps the first place to check is where our doubt meter is in the promises of God. They are not foolish to believe, mere pipe dreams. They are His commitments to us. The world won't keep its promises. God will.

And after the promises come the instructions. Thank Jesus, God is a God who tells us exactly what to do. The promises are from Him *to* us; the instructions are from Him *for* us, and they are all in this same passage. Let us not think we can claim the promises of God and live ignoring the instructions, for it is a marriage of the two. Jesus promises us things and asks us to do things at the same time. It is a mutual effort, with a divine hierarchy—God over us. And aren't we glad it is, since for us to be in charge would be a complete disaster.

God's instructions precisely:

> Think clearly and exercise self-control. Look forward to the gracious salvation that will come to you when Jesus Christ is revealed to the world. So you must live as God's obedient children. Don't slip back into your old ways of living to satisfy your own desires. You didn't know any better then. But now you must be holy in everything you do, just as God who chose you is holy. For the Scriptures say, "You must be holy because I am holy."

> And remember that the heavenly Father to whom you pray has no favorites. He will judge or reward you according to what you do. So you must live in reverent fear of him during your time here as "foreigners in the land." For you know that God paid a ransom to save you from the empty life you inherited from your ancestors. And the ransom he paid with mere gold or silver. It was the precious blood of Christ, the sinless, spotless Lamb of God. God chose him as your ransom long before the world began, but now he has revealed him to you in these last days.

> Through Christ you have come to trust in God. And you have placed your faith and hope in God because he raised Christ from the dead and gave him great glory.

> You were cleansed from your sins when you obeyed the

truth, so now you must show sincere love to each other as brothers and sisters. Love each other deeply with all your heart (1 Peter 1:13-22).

**Prepare, present, and practice.** This is what Jesus tells us now to do. We *prepare* our minds and our lives to exercise self-control. We *present* ourselves to Him as holy. We *practice* these things we know and He tells us in His Word, over and over again. We've talked about all of these things in our declarations in the chapters: preparing our minds and lives is putting on the warrior boots of standard—knowing what we believe and telling the truth. Presenting ourselves to God is offering warrior boots of strength of rising up and going on record in faith, with all the love and dedication to a God who has given His life for us, and we then offer back a pure and holy life. We practice these things by choosing Him over and over again, following Him closely—moving back when we move away and staying in tight. These are the instructions. They are clear and simple, strong and beautiful.

In our everyday life, here's the picture…

*Prepare:* No longer winging it spiritually as a viable option. Instead, choosing to live with a heart-led, fully engaged mind and body spiritual strategy. All in.

*Present:* Open-door policy with God, no more secret life. Living with the goal to hand back to Him a clean and holy life, never taking advantage of His grace, freely given. (Interesting, isn't it, that *present* can also be pronounced *pre-sent*, which means both gift and staying right there?)

*Practice:* Once is not enough. Last year at that conference is not enough. Daily. Over and over again, we trust God; we follow God; we choose God.

These promises and instructions are God's tool for readiness in us. We need them; we love them; we live them or we cave.

---

*The Bible is simultaneously as deep as the deepest well and as accessible as the nearest bucket.*

---

## Staying Sober

Today I want to cave.

I read an article this morning that messed me up and now all I can do is stare blankly at this screen, hoping to write something that makes sense. Nik Ripkin's article "An Eerie, Unacceptable Silence" is about the Western Church and how we stay silent about how other believers, martyrs, in the wider Church, the Kingdom of God, forsake all for the gospel…while we sit in our comfortable first-world spiritual life.[2]

And as I sit here at a desk with Christian sayings on plaques around me, my closed Bible mere inches away, in an air-conditioned house with a pantry of food stocked full, I know it is me who doesn't have a clue, me who is soft, me who needs a huge dose of reality. Today I am overwhelmed by the reality of a society of Christian cute—driven by our Christian tweets and inspirational sayings and jewelry we mostly just wear but don't live. Our complaint after complaint about everything under the sun, being so very proud of ourselves for our short bursts of being faithful to the Lord.

There is fire within us, God's Holy Spirit if we are born again, and yet we keep it well contained. We don't want to be too radical. We want to be accepted and keep having all the regular fun. We've got to stop thinking this way or very soon we won't know what a true follower of Jesus really looks like at all. It gets harder to identify one every day. There is little about us that is set apart and different.

The world is volatile and we are crazy weary of it, and many are preaching a message to *love, just love*, and our hearts long for this because love is God, and all of creation, whether we know it or not, aches in our bones for Him and, as a result, His peace. So now in our weariness of volatility we are running, running farther and farther from the mess, wildly and without compass, so desperate to just get away from it all that we have left behind important things like truth and commitment to holiness and righteousness.

I think, to survive, we've got to stop being shocked by the world and exchange it for being shocked by our own willingness to be like it. If we are to have angst at this moment, let it be because we see the realities of how we are not yet like Christ.

Jesus told us over and over again in the Word, warned us, left us the promises and instructions as to what to do when all that's happening, happens. It's time to get over the shock about how bad it is out there and instead warrior up. We won't wish our world back into being okay. We can and should pray for full repentance and restoration, no matter the symptoms and fears. But we won't do ourselves or anyone else any good by continually being surprised every time an evil in this world crops up. Let it be known: the only hope for this world is if it turns to God. Otherwise, we haven't heard or seen anything yet.

> *If we are to have angst at this moment,*
> *let it be because we see the realities*
> *of how we are not yet like Christ.*

Satan is so sly that he uses underground tactics to hurt us while we are unaware. He dresses things up (including himself—2 Corinthians 11:14 tells us, "Even Satan disguises himself as an angel of light") and calls them something different, and it's nearly impossible to distinguish between the two. Lest we think there's not a more underground strategy of the evil one to the chaos on the world—that it all just blew up overnight unexpectedly and now we are left cleaning up the mess of a suddenly broken world—know that it is no accident that the world is mean and cruel. The world unrest—political tensions, murder, sexual deviancy, destitution, abuse—is not just a byproduct of a fallen world. The calculation of Satan has everything to do with it. He's convinced believers to ride the middle, to be so weary of the mess that all we want to do is either run wildly far, far away or go to sleep and shut our eyes so we don't have to deal with it. We are so tired of meanness and intolerance that all we want is peace and love, ironically, God-only things that are right wants. And while we wish the mess away, God wants to use it to transform and change us as we press harder into Him.

Because truth and holiness are often bold and hard, it is easy for Satan to dress them up and sell them as meanness and intolerance. He has figured out a way to make them look exactly alike, though they aren't. Satan has stood them up in front of us, looking so authentic in their costumed guise, and whispered, *This is meanness and intolerance…you don't want any part of them*, and then slyly slinked away. And we are left blinking back tears, looking at a couple we don't want to become standing in front of us, feeling like the only way to avoid keeping their company is either to stop talking altogether or join the crowd shouting loudly against them. The problem is: they aren't the right target. They are right and true things, dressed up by Satan to make us think they are the things they are not. And the voice of Christianity grows weaker and weaker in all its confusion and fear.

Without truth there is no repentance or turning back to God, the answer to the unrest of this world. Without holiness there is no revival. It's all a ploy of Satan for Christians to have diminishing influence and finally just go away. Stay sober to this ploy, my friends. He can only silence us if we choose to stay unaware and unprepared.

Staying sober is the only way. Staying sober to the disguises and the underground strategy and the goal of the crippling fears. If Satan can persuade us our strong stance for God will equal marginalization or being misunderstood, he can usually stop us from our obedience to God because the human heart is frail and needy of acceptance. *Stay sober to this.* The struggle is real.

Stay sober to the trap of falling into worshipping all around God but never God Himself—these statements of self-help that leave God out but tug at our heart strings…the doing-good mentality without knowing the Good Shepherd Himself. It's pantheism. The world won't call it that. They will call it love. They will call it karma and doing good. Satan knows you won't fall for pantheism if it's called that, so he dresses it up.

Stay sober to the entrapment of misunderstanding freedom in Christ as the go-ahead to do things that will hamper your holiness. So many times we abuse that freedom by calling it our right and doing things that don't keep us alert and sober. My friend, I don't judge you for what you may choose to do. My addiction to *People* magazine and reality TV can be just as harmful as yours to porn in the way it distances me from God. What we each do that doesn't help our holiness is just distraction preference and logistics. When we have our nose in worldly idols, we are compromised away from being alert and aware. When hard things happen, we are all awakened from the same nap—people in the same dead sleep. Now our goal is not to fall back asleep until the next time, the next thing. We can choose to hear this as legalism or we can choose to see it as guardrails that save our lives. Christian shells with hollow insides blow over easily. Be sober, friends. Stay sober to misunderstanding freedom.

Stay sober when you encounter Christian prosperity speech and favor-heavy theology. More Jesus followers with servant credibility and a steadied track record of gospel purity, less Christian celebrity and Christian cute, please. It's going to take a whole lot more warrior strength than that.

Stay sober to the reality that the belief that God owes us the life we conjure up in our minds is a way the enemy keeps us self-focused, entitled, and estranged from God when He doesn't let us have our way. When God says, *But what if that's not My plan for your life?* there is nothing to answer but *okay.* Satan wants us to spend our whole life in a whirlpool of resisting.

There's a call to stay sober now, as there was a call to stay sober in Bible times. God's call is always for us to be sober because He knows that in our sobriety we cling to Him as the only hope of survival and preparation. The book of Joel spends the first 37 verses with sobering straight talk, mentioning locust infestation, the death of a loved one, farmers ruined crops, famine, confused cows, miserable bleating sheep, fire, lack of water, blackness, clouds, and earthquakes as references to illustrate all the devastation that is to come, lest they wake up to their compromise and sin. The people of Judah were in an identical place to where we are now—the need to turn to God every bit as dire.

And yet, praise be to God who brings good news, because every time there's a sobering talk of sin and judgment, there's a promise of hope and rescue at the next turn. Were we to focus too heavily on either (the judgment or the rescue), we might despair or live recklessly. But in our lives, it is a healthy awareness of both. As always, the Christian life is a life of checks and balances, with God's mercy being the greatest gift of them all.

And in that eighteenth verse in Joel 2, after all the hard, straight talk that is meant to lead to contriteness but could be turned by humans into inward despair…the restoration talk begins.

> Then the LORD will pity his people
>     and jealously guard the honor of his land.
> The LORD will reply,
> "Look! I am sending you grain and new wine and olive oil,
>     enough to satisfy your needs.
> You will no longer be an object of mockery
>     among the surrounding nations.
> I will drive away these armies from the north.
>     I will send them into the parched wastelands.
> Those in the front will be driven into the Dead Sea,
>     and those at the rear into the Mediterranean.
> The stench of their rotting bodies will rise over the land."
> Surely the LORD has done great things!
>     Don't be afraid, my people.
> Be glad now and rejoice,
>     for the Lord has done great things.

Don't be afraid, you animals of the field,
 for the wilderness pastures will soon be green.
The trees will again be filled with fruit;
 fig trees and grapevines will be loaded down once more.
Rejoice, you people of Jerusalem!
 Rejoice in the LORD your God!
For the rain he sends demonstrates his faithfulness.
 Once more the autumn rains will come,
 as well as the rains of spring.
The threshing floors will again be piled high with grain,
 and the presses will overflow with new wine and olive oil.
The LORD says, "I will give you back what you lost
 to the swarming locusts, the hopping locusts,
the stripping locusts, and the cutting locusts.
 It was I who sent this great destroying army against you.
Once again you will have all the food you want,
 and you will praise the LORD your God,
who does these miracles for you.
 Never again will my people be disgraced.
Then you will know that I am among my people Israel,
 that I am the LORD your God, and there is no other.
Never again will my people be disgraced (verses 18-27).

The relief for our sin and disobedience comes in the beautiful restoration—after confession, after a turning back to God. It's opportunity, every second of every minute of every day. We never stop being called back to a place of spiritual sobriety, and we never lose the opportunity for rehabilitation: with Jesus leading the charge for both. New wine, restored reputation, enemies driven away, no more fear, green pastures, rejoicing, a giving back of all that has been taken away by our own choosing. Yes, indeed, the rain may seem like rain, but it is really the expression of His faithfulness. Only God can send rain and turn it into grace.

I don't believe we mean to lose sight of things and not stay sober. I don't think we mean to slip slide away. It's just easy to do in a world that wants us to pull away from God. We get careless, self-absorbed, and forgetful. Right now is a good time to tell God this and then ask Him for help.

It is my prayer now…the same as Joel in 3:11: *"O Lord, call out your warriors!"*

And when He calls, may it be our answer back, *Yes, Lord, I am here.*

---

*While we wish the mess away, God wants to use it to transform and change us as we press harder into Him.*

---

## Declare

Our spiritual life will only be as strong as the commitment to our declarations. We believe them; we speak them over our life; we live them out. It's not enough to just say we want to live with a different strategy. Lots of unsuccessful people do that. We have to implement the strategy, every day of our lives.

*I am able:* the first and important declaration of knowing our right and privilege to be strong and steady, through God—no matter what.

*I will know what I believe:* the declaration to be grounded in our convictions. We may hear a lot of noise in the world, but we know what we believe and don't waver from it.

*I will tell the truth:* the declaration to be honest with ourselves and share the truth with others. We may be tempted to shy away from truth, but we choose it over the secrecy and deceit that lead to death.

*I will rise up and stand firm:* the declaration of our boots of strength first course of action. We may tremble in our hearts, but we rise up, stand firm, and let our convictions be known.

*I will go on record:* the declaration, which seals the deal. We will not shrink back, but with wisdom and strength, we will speak up for God.

*I will choose God:* the declaration that we will always, no matter what, choose God. We choose God forever, because He is worth it and we won't be able to survive without Him.

*I will follow God forever:* the declaration that our lives will consistently stay with Him. He knows the way, and we will follow Him forever.

*I am ready:* the final declaration of the warrior boots life. We are ready, because of Jesus. He will help us live the Jesus strong life.

We are able to do this, we are ready to do this, always and only because of Jesus. Don't ever let anyone tell you differently, including Satan who wants most to get you discouraged and off track. Be stronger than that. Be sober to that. Nothing he says changes the reality of how it is. Don't ever believe his empty, hot air. Ability is not contingent upon bravery. Ability is the reality for every believer, right now. Readiness is not found in an undisturbed life. It is found in a life that is grounded and prepared in the midst of chaos.

We are ready, friends. We are able. Storms are headed our way; this is not the time to shrink back. "Do not throw away this confidence...do not draw back," says Hebrews 10:35 and 39. There is nothing in this world that can take a child of God down—not the hardest of life, the excruciating pain of loss and death. Our feelings do not own space in the solidity of God's promises. So park your life in the truth of the Word and do not ever pull away.

We survive and live a beautiful life like this: we prepare for this life by fortifying our heart and mind. We present ourselves to God, every day, for strength and recalibration. We practice our declarations, over and over again. There is nothing extravagant to this strategy, but there is also no shortcut. We who do not waver from the strategy of God for our survival will be the ones still standing when the winds blow the others away. Life with God is not short bursts of faithful; it is the long obedience. It is the Galatians 5 life where no one can run us off course. "Despite storms, despite waiting, despite hard days…they go right on producing delicious fruit." This, my fellow journeyers, is the goal.

> Blessed are those who trust in the LORD
>> and have made the LORD their hope and confidence.
> They are like trees planted along a riverbank,
>> with roots that reach deep into the water.
> Such trees are not bothered by the heat
>> or worried by long months of drought.
> Their leaves stay green,
>> and they never stop producing fruit (Jeremiah 17:7-8).

*Only God can send rain and turn it into grace.*

This is a crazy, undeniable promise—that no matter how long the drought of relief from whatever pains us, we can still live well. I want to be a fruit producer. I want my leaves to stay green, despite conditions around me over which I have no control. I want hope. I want confidence. I want to be a warrior and not a wimp.

So I will declare things over my life and I will walk them out, every day. I will not turn my head to the right or to the left, but I will keep locked eye contact with God. He will lead me. He will hold my arms as I buckle from weak knees walking in a hard world. Walking Jesus strong will not take me becoming a super human; it will take me being a weak human strengthened by the mighty, unending power of God.

I declare this today. It is the fearlessness in you and me He's calling out.

## Let's Go

It helps me to know you are with me.

We can do this alone with just God, and He will be enough. Yet He set it up so we would wear our warrior boots together, march loudly to the Savior's gospel song. There is strength in our togetherness. We can remind each other of the truth when the noise gets extra loud, help buoy each other when the winds get extra strong and the waves threaten to carry us away. Many pairs of warrior boots marching strongly together are the sound of the Church in its greatest effectiveness. The army of God. The servants of God. The adopted kids. Together, the warriors.

I'm ready to go…Are you? When we choose God…know what we believe…commit to stand in what we believe…and truly trust God, we are ready, like never before, to put our warrior boots on and live as a confident, strong, steady believer in Jesus Christ. It is what will influence the world for good. It is what will change our life forever. It is what we need, what we want, what will be the missing piece to the faith walk we are on anytime we don't feel secure.

We are ready to face a dark world with an internal light that will not be squelched. We are ready to live a life of consistency and a ministry of sameness, to rise to the reputation of being fearless. We are ready to speak hard truth and not worry about acceptance in the eyes of others. We draw people to the strength within us that God supplies and live with a different perspective and conviction, that no matter what comes our way, the absolutes of our life will not change. How amazing is this, that we are ready for it?

It's our heart, our craving, to feel prepared and ready for a hard life, yet most of us settle for a few good days. Let's not settle anymore. There's no need. With Jesus, this security we want is possible. We won't live our life being perfectly fear- and doubt-free, and troubles will still come, sometimes just here and there and sometimes in overwhelming spades. But we will be grounded. Imagine going through your life without being so very tossed about by what others choose to do. Imagine living with a perspective that the world's mess can't touch. Imagine emotional security. Imagine a steadfast mind. This is the life of a warrior boots believer, and we are ready for it, right now.

Putting our warrior boots on is crucial so we can lead others—help the world know truth, find Jesus so they can maneuver through life and find a level of joy on earth—which is the call of God on our life, by the way. That is the second most important aspect to us living the warrior boots life. The first is about us, because we cannot give out what we ourselves do not have, as we talked about before. It is about our own heart and soul and yes, even physical preparation (taking proper care of our bodies) to be so solid with Jesus that we stop retreating, taking ourselves out of the game, and being gripped with fear so much so that we live like our unsaved neighbors who do not know Hope. We have to look different or they won't reach for us. The light has to be bright so they will be drawn in. We will have no clout if we ask other people to love and trust God when we ourselves do not.

*I know*. It is our human tendency to preach but not live, and this is why we are not consistently gospel effective. *We know*. But still we worry. *We believe*. But still we doubt. But at a certain point it has to become more about where we want to go than what keeps us from it. No more excuses. No more lamenting over circumstances we can't control. No more trying to pretend the crazy of our lives away. Forward, onward, walking strong. He told us what to do: *Get yourself ready and go.*

Be prepared. Have our eyes fully open. Know what we believe. Stay firm. Run into His arms. Lead people to know Him. Live as He lived and love as He loves and as the world gets scarier and more and more people become afraid, be the one they run to because they know that although we are not perfect, we live above the mess and will tell them the truth. This will make them curious. This will make them want to know how to live better too.

He said it all throughout Scripture, and He says it now, in the exact same place: to *prepare, prepare, prepare* for what is to come and in the authority in which He has given us. Be the kind of people who represent hope and steadiness and strength, not panic and insecurity. "No one lights a lamp and puts it in a place where it will be hidden, or under a bowl. Instead they put it on its stand, so that those who come in may see the light" (Luke 11:33 NIV). The beauty of the truth and security that Jesus offers, do not keep hidden. You know the cure for life. Do not keep it to yourself. Share it so that your life on earth will be glorified in heaven and many will come to know Christ because of you. Share your prayers. Share your love. Share your light. Share your life. Help lead other people when it gets dark. This is the only real, fulfilling life, all of this goodness and giving away.

How else would we want to live? What else would we rather do with our life—collect things that don't wind up meaning a thing, gather stuff that eventually ruins, run ourselves in circles until we die and no one even remembers we used to be here on earth too? No to that. No to everything that is not of God.

Jesus knew and knows still, we would need to prepare for this tough world—have our warrior boots on—because without them, we would attempt to navigate in flimsy soles. Preparation is not the calculation of man; it is the genius of God. He told us in Ephesians 6 so very plainly: exactly what to do and how to do it and even why, because He knew otherwise, when Satan turned up the clever, we would punch without power...dodge arrows without agility... white-knuckle it through trials and keep grasping for hope instead of living in the stance of holy offense: strong, steady, ready, and sure.

The glorious thing happens when we live with the discipline of preparation: we stop being so exhausted. Our attempts begin to seem ineffective and eventually we put them away because we have no need of them anymore. We have our warrior boots on. We have been strengthened and prepared by God, and He is readying us for the storms and the mountains—the hilly terrain we cannot navigate ourselves. Only then can we be used by God to help lead other people out of the dark.

None of us come into our spiritual life being warriors. This is why God spent so much time in the Word telling us to ready our hearts. We come soft and develop grit. Sometimes being a warrior looks like boldness. Sometimes the most warrior-like thing we can do is rest. Always it looks like a strong, whole heart. Without that, we won't be anything, ever, at all.

And lest, even in this moment, you have begun to retreat into your insecurity that you don't have what it takes...please remember this: we don't have to feel ready, today. I trust and pray this book has nudged us to a readiness place, infused strength that comes from the truth of the Word into our bones, helped us fall more in love with Jesus, the Help. We have the Spirit of God within us to make us into the warriors we never thought we could be. Remember, we will never just one day wake up warriors. We will prepare for the day we need to become one and find we already are.

*Put your warrior boots on:* our rally, our call to be heart and life prepared.

It's time. Things have gotten dark. People around us are freaking out.

We can't close our eyes and plug our ears to the things we need to know.

Life is really just about one thing and one thing only: God. It is always going to be about God. It is only going to be about God. It is forever going to be about God.

Other fools can try to take His place, but it will always, always be Him. Even those powerful kings, the most powerful political people, the smartest, the richest, the most famous in all of the world one day will bow. This is our God, Him or nothing.

> God never negotiates with men. Jesus Christ's death on the cross put an end to any kind of negotiations. It is now Christ or nothing. It is now God's Word in its entirety or nothing (A. W. Tozer).[3]

Every time we hear bad news and start to panic: remember God. In Him, we find our center. In Him, we find our strength. In Him, who has the last word.

> And that about wraps it up. God is strong, and he wants you strong. So take everything the Master has set out for you, well-made weapons of the best materials. And put them to use so you will be able to stand up to everything the Devil throws your way. This is no afternoon athletic contest that we'll walk away from and forget about in a couple of hours. This is for keeps, a life-or-death fight to the finish against the Devil and all his angels.
>
> Be prepared. You're up against far more than you can handle on your own. Take all the help you can get, every weapon God has issued, so that when it's all over but the shouting you'll still be on your feet. Truth, righteousness, peace, faith, and salvation are more than words. Learn how to apply them. You'll need them throughout your life. God's Word is an indispensable weapon. In the same way, prayer is essential in this ongoing warfare. Pray hard and long. Pray for your brothers and sisters. Keep your eyes open. Keep each other's spirits up so that no one falls behind or drops out.
>
> And don't forget to pray for me (Ephesians 6:10-19 MSG).

Pray for me, friends. I will pray for you. Pray we will choose the warrior boots life. Pray we can walk Jesus strong, even today. Pray we will commit to the declarations. Pray we will know we are able, and we are ready.

One day we will start our real best life and all get better. Warrior up, ready ones. That day is not yet here.

# I AM READY

**Take a Deeper Dive:** Joel 2; 1 Peter 1:1-12

**10 minutes:** Welcome. Share about a time when you didn't think you were ready for something but did it anyway, and it turned out good or better than you thought (funny or serious).

**10 Minutes:** Intro to chapter through Video Teaching with Lisa (outline and videos available online at www.warriorbootsbooks.com)

**35 Minutes:** Small Group Discussion (Take the first 10 minutes to answer privately, then the last 25 to discuss as a group.)

1. Can you relate to her feelings of life in general, walking anyway despite all the hard?

2. How do you feel about the promises of God? Which in your life have you been the most grateful for?

3. Lisa outlines the instructions of God in 1 Peter 1: prepare, present, practice. At which point in this process do you see believers often breaking down? How does that hinder them?

4. What do the words *staying sober* mean to you?

5. Of the eight declarations we looked at in the book, which one causes you the most difficulty? How can making declarations in your life help you?

6. Do you believe you have a life of a victor? Are you

currently living that life? What's in your way and how can you change that?

**Prayer:** God, we claim the truth that we are ready to walk Jesus strong in this difficult world only because of You. We ask for Your strength and wisdom and guidance. We ask for the courage to walk anyway, whether we feel strong or not. Help us stay sober to the ways of the devil and prepare, present, and practice our faith to honor You. Thank You for giving us the life of the victor through Your Son's death on the cross. We offer our lives to You, now and always. Yes and amen.

**Bonus Home Helps:**

1. Do a word study of *ready* from Scripture.

2. Memorize and meditate on 1 Peter 1:5: "Through your faith, God is protecting you by his power until you receive this salvation."

3. Take one day to study and think about the words *prepare*, *present*, and *practice*. Ask a close person to you if they see you doing those three things and if not, which ones need work. Do the same for your friend. Pray together that you both will walk stronger in this moving forward.

4. Buy two small canvases and paints and create art pieces of the eight declarations we have studied in this book and hang them on the way into your home so you can always see them. (Or do some type of art to help you remember them.) Artistic ability is not important. When you finish, make another as a gift for someone else.

5. Ask someone close to you to pray for you to claim your life of a victor and live out this three-word (*I Am Ready*) declaration in your life.

BONUS BLOG POST:

# PUT YOUR WARRIOR BOOTS ON

September 4, 2015

I sit here this morning, feeling less like a warrior and more like a tired woman who doesn't want to hear any more of the world's bad news.

The bed calls me, the covers promise comfort, and it all seems perfect because it's just another normal day and *I'm grown and can do what I want.*

But the truth is, mostly I'm just afraid. Mostly I'm just trying to pretend away the realities of this world and get rid of that stupid knot that's in my stomach from the things I read in my early-morning scroll of Facebook.

Killing babies, killing cops, killing Christians, Miley telling our kids, "Yeah, I smoke pot" like it's the perfect idea, and musician after musician on an awards show all but having sex on stage. I'm equipped to fix none of it, because *who can fight such madness unless they are God and the last I checked I'm not Him?* Early-morning helplessness feels especially cruel when a day is supposed to hold promise.

*I just want it all to stop.* I want to be able to have fun and not hear hard things. I want to be able to compartmentalize faith where it worships neatly in church but doesn't have to wear combat boots. I'm a wimp, I tell you. Yes, if not wanting to live in a *world where I will have trouble* (see John 16:33) is wimpy, then of course I'm a wimp. I want the hut on the tropical clear blue water with the fruity drink and my people for the rest of my life and *poof*, this all goes away. That's what I want.

But I know (and sometimes this makes me mad) that being a wimp is not my option. When I committed to Christ, I committed to a soul battle, the highest cause. So as much as I want to be absorbed into crowds, this is not the Jesus-following life.

Even as I pull the covers up to my neck to make the escape, I hear these words in my head, *Lead me to the Rock that is higher than I.* And I remember Psalm 61:2. And I know my life is not in escaping but in following my Leader. It's not in retreating but being equipped.

The world will either eat my lunch or I will combat it. Evil will either make me a wimp or a warrior. These are the only two choices, and I can't change that no matter how hard I try. Only God can make me a warrior. And so, I rally, but not because I'm ready. I rally because warriors don't wait for a perfect day to get prepared.

- **I will know what I believe.** I will not believe everything because believing everything really means believing nothing. And we have plenty of people believing nothing already.

- **I will stand in what I believe.** I will choose God, over and over again, because every day this is what it will require. I know that choosing nothing is really choosing everything, and God is the Only Everything.

- **I will share what I believe.** I will go on record. I will be vocal in conviction and not pride. And if the truth I share offends others, I will share still, as God leads me.

- **I will trust God.** I will trust Him, forever and ever, even when, even if, always. I will trust God in the bad news. I will trust God through the madness. I will trust God without asking Him to do what I want so I can trust Him more.

Today, I will put on my warrior boots. I do it to be prepared. I do it to survive. I do it because I have no other option. I do it because I belong to Jesus.

And even in my fear, I will climb to the Rock that is higher than I so He can hold me, heal me, pull me out from under the covers where I hide, and make me into His strong warrior.

I will. *I will.*

# ACKNOWLEDGMENTS

No duty is more urgent than
that of returning thanks.

**JAMES ALLEN**

Scotty, I love you. For 21 years, you've pursued my heart even when I haven't known how to properly open it. You're my faithful, safe place.

Graham, Micah, and Shae: My darlings, Jesus is the only thing in life. That's all I can tell you. You'll need these warrior boots, more than you may now know. Never forget to put them on or that your mom loves you, forever.

Mom and Dad: You still take care of me, every day, with your cheers and prayers. Your constancy in my life is among my greatest joy and your greatest legacy.

Colleen: Your friendship has saved me. Our 9:00 a.m. phone calls wrote most of this book. I know God loves me because He gave me you.

Wendy, Heather, Myquillin, Mary, Sarah, Kelly, Michele, Kathryn, Suzie, MaryBeth, Shari, Dena, Lisa—my closest girl tribe. Some of you are my every days, some are my every weeks, and some are whenever we can make it happen. You are the girls who keep me sane and get my most honest texts (okay, sometimes *novels*). Thank you for knowing who I am. I know who you are too, and I choose you.

Reimers and Whittles: Each of you brings something important to my life. Thank you, loving in-laws, sibs, and offspring. I love you.

Jana Burson: God connections, right timing, and like hearts. These things and a shared love of football are the things I thank God for when I remember you, agent and friend.

Kathleen Kerr: You've labored with me through yet another book. Is there some sort of Olympic medal for this? There should be. Thank you for a heart of gold, a fast wit, and an iron-sharpening commitment. This is your book too, as was *I Want God*.

Harvest House: I am at home with you. Bob Hawkins Jr., you are an astute president and a generous friend. Thank you for valuing people and loving God. Your humble leadership is what makes this house great. LaRae Weikert, you're consistently one of the best people I've ever met. Thank you for your joy, strength, and unwavering belief in me.

Mel and Jay Stewart, Teri Furr, Watchman Nee, A. W. Tozer, Elisabeth Elliot, Monty Hipp, Bob Sorge, Samuel Brengle, Henri Nouwen, Christy Nockels, John Eldredge, Francis Chan, and Angela Mitchell—those who have appearances in this book: When you write a book, you realize the people who currently influence your life and words. You are those people. Thank you for being faithful teachers.

Reader friends, friends I meet as I travel and speak, online friends I connect with nearly every day…you may never know how much you impact me, but you do. Your faces and stories flash in my mind when I want to quit. Your encouragement dries days of tears. You've blessed me as much as I've ever blessed you.

Jesus Christ, it's always been You. It will always be You. I dream of our face-to-face.

# NOTES

## Introduction
1. Samuel Brengle, *Take Time to Be Holy* (Carol Stream, IL: Tyndale Momentum, 2013), np.

## 1. I Am Able
1. John Eldredge, *Walking with God* (Nashville, Tennessee: Thomas Nelson, 2008), 129.
2. Despite my best efforts, I have been unable to find a source for this quotation.
3. Watchman Nee, *Sit, Walk, Stand* (Carol Stream, Illinois: Tyndale House, 1977), 58.

## 2. I Will Know What I Believe
1. Cardinal John Henry Newman, *The Works of Cardinal Newman* (Minneapolis, MN: University of Minnesota, 1913), 184.
2. Charles H. Spurgeon, *The Metropolitan Tabernacle Pulpit: Volume 33 Sermons Preached and Revised During the Year 1887* (Carlisle, PA: Banner of Truth Trust, 1969), 489.
3. St. Augustine, quoted in Lloyd Cory, *Quote, Unquote* (Wheaton, IL: Victor Books, 1977), 197.
4. Despite my best efforts, I have been unable to find a source for this quotation.
5. A.W. Tozer, *The Pursuit of God* (Ventura, CA: Gospel Light Publishers, 2013), np.

## 3. I Will Tell the Truth
1. Anne Lamott, Twitter post, August 21, 2016, 7:44 a.m., twitter.com/annelamott.
2. A. W. Tozer, *The Pursuit of God*, np.

## 4. I Will Rise Up and Stand Firm
1. A. W. Tozer, *The Pursuit of God*
2. Bob Sorge, *Secrets of the Secret Place* (Grandview, MO: Oasis House, 2001), 32.
3. I recommend Francis Chan's book *You and Me Forever* for further discussion on this topic.
4. Watchman Nee, *Sit, Walk, Stand*, 53.
5. John Eldredge, *Walking with God*, np.
6. Despite my best efforts, I have been unable to find a source for this quotation.

## 5. I Will Go on Record
1. Samuel Brengle, *Take Time to Be Holy*, 40.

## 6. I Will Choose God
1. Francis Chan, *You and Me Forever* (San Francisco, CA: Claire Love Publishing, 2014), 151, 157.
2. Aaron Sorkin, "Take Out the Trash Day," *The West Wing*, episode 13, season 1, directed by Ken Olin, aired January 26, 2000, NBC.
3. James MacDonald, "God's Moral Will" (online devotional), March 7, 2012, http://www.jamesmacdonald.com/teaching/devotionals/2012-03-07/.

## 7. I Will Follow God Forever
1. Henri Nouwen, *The Inner Voice of Love* (New York: Image by Doubleday, 1998), 8.

## 8. I Am Ready
1. *Life Application Study Bible,* New Living Translation (Wheaton, IL: Tyndale House Publishers, 1996), commentary on 1 Peter 1:1.
2. Nik Ripkin, "An Eerie, Unacceptable Silence," *Desiring God*, July 16, 2016, http://www.desiringgod.org/articles/an-eerie-unacceptable-silence.
3. A.W. Tozer, *God's Power for Your Life* (Bloomington, MN: Bethany House Publishers, 2013), np.

# ABOUT LISA WHITTLE

*Jesus is everything.* It is the heart, the passion and the leadership approach of author and speaker, Lisa Whittle. As the daughter of a pastor, Lisa's longest community is with the Church, which has become her greatest place of ministry. Her love runs deep to see people pursue Jesus for life, grow deep roots of faith, and walk strong in the midst of a world that so often seems to have gone crazy.

For this reason, Lisa has dedicated her life to writing and speaking about the truth of Jesus Christ and how wanting Him the most changes everything. Lisa is the author of five—soon to be six—books and a sought-out Bible teacher for her wit and bold, bottom-line approach. Her *with you-for you* signature style is a favorite of audiences who have her coming back to speak into them year after year. From retreats to rehab facilities to college campuses to the large church or conference stage, Lisa's desire remains the same: to point people to the Jesus who can change their life.

Lisa's books include:

- *Put Your Warrior Boots On:* Walking Jesus Strong, Once and for All

- *5 Word Prayers: Where to Start When You Don't Know What to Say to God* (coming soon)

- *I Want God:* Forever Changed by the Revival of Your Soul

- *{w}hole:* An Honest Look at the Holes in Your Life and How to Let God Fill Them

- *Behind Those Eyes:* What's Really Going on Inside the Souls of Women

- *The 7 Hardest Things God Asks a Woman to Do*

In addition to speaking, media appearances and writing online, Lisa has done master's work in marriage and family counseling and advocated for Compassion International. Wife, mom, and lover of laughter, good food, her fluffy dog, interior design, and the Bible, Lisa is a grateful work in progress. You can find her on Facebook (Lisa Whittle), follow her on Instagram (@LisaWhittle) and Twitter (@LisaRWhittle), and visit her ministry community at www.lisawhittle.com.

# ALSO BY LISA WHITTLE

### *I Want God*

It is in the heart of every person to want God, but life gets loud and we forget Him. We get consumed by our problems, our desires, ourselves. We forget our first encounter with the Savior and how much we once wanted Him...the way we believed He could use our life...the fulfillment He provides that everyday life cannot.

A guidebook, a teacher and a resource, all in one, *I Want God* brings rich simplicity to life-altering principles. With her signature boldness and raw authenticity, author and speaker Lisa Whittle inspires with bottom-line truth about what happens when life gets off track and how to find our way back to the God we want most.

To learn more about Harvest House books and
to read sample chapters, visit our website:

**www.harvesthousepublishers.com**

HARVEST HOUSE PUBLISHERS
EUGENE, OREGON